Red, White, and Blue on the Runway

Red, White, and Blue on the Runway

The 1968 White House Fashion Show and the Politics of American Style

★ Kimberly Chrisman-Campbell

The Kent State University Press ▣ Kent, Ohio

ISBN 978-1-60635-432-2
Manufactured in the United States of America

Cataloging information for this title is available at the Library of Congress.

26 25 24 23 22   5 4 3 2 1

Contents

Preface

On February 29, 1968, the White House hosted its first—and only—fashion show. While this historic event has been virtually forgotten today, it received extensive and glowing coverage in the mainstream and fashion media at the time. Organizers and journalists even predicted that it would become an annual event—a permanent fixture on the American fashion calendar along with Press Week and the Party of the Year, now known as New York Fashion Week and the Met Gala, respectively.

But the first White House fashion show was destined to be the last. To illuminate why this PR stunt turned into a PR disaster, this study reconstructs the event—and its political fallout—using eyewitness accounts and carefully preserved records, images, and artifacts from the Lyndon B. Johnson Presidential Library and other museum and archival collections. Together, they tell a cautionary tale illustrating the perennial dangers of mixing fashion and politics and chart the evolution of American style from the postwar period to the counterculture revolution.

By an accident of history, the unapologetically patriotic event occurred at a precarious time for the nation. The year 1968 has gone down in American history as one of unrest and upheaval. Much of the social and political turmoil we now associate with "the sixties" actually took place in that single year. During 1968, we saw the assassinations of Martin Luther King Jr. and Senator Robert F. Kennedy. In Vietnam, it was the year of the Tet Offensive, the My Lai massacre, and Associated Press photographer Eddie Adams's photo of General Nguyen Ngoc Loan executing a Viet Cong prisoner on a Saigon street. Johnny Cash performed at Folsom Prison. Arthur Ashe became the first Black man to win the US Open.

The Boeing 747 made its maiden voyage. Moviegoers could choose from *Rosemary's Baby*, *Barbarella*, *Funny Girl*, and *Planet of the Apes*; *Hair* opened on Broadway. Mrs. Kennedy became Mrs. Onassis. The Beatles released *The White Album*. The Zodiac Killer claimed his first victims. In America and around the world, populist uprisings turned into violent street battles. Student protests rocked Paris and Mexico City, where American athletes Tommie Smith and John Carlos raised their fists in a Black Power salute at the Olympics. *Star Trek* delivered television's first interracial kiss.

In the grand scheme of things, it is perhaps not surprising that a self-congratulatory celebration of Seventh Avenue—staged as part of a ladies' luncheon—did not make the immediate splash its organizers hoped for, much less evoke fond memories more than half a century later. Yet 1968 was also a pivotal year for the fashion world. Calvin Klein, Anne Klein, Halston, and Stephen Burrows launched their game-changing labels. British couturier Hardy Amies designed the far-out costumes for *2001: A Space Odyssey*. Yves Saint Laurent's safari jacket was spotted in the wilds of French *Vogue*; perhaps not coincidentally, Balenciaga closed his house, declaring that haute couture was dead. At the Miss America pageant, protestors tossed girdles and bras into a symbolic "freedom trash can." You didn't have to be a dedicated follower of fashion to sense that change was in the air—not just the usual seasonal cycle of fashion but seismic shifts in values, ambitions, and morals.

The Baby Boom had produced a "youthquake"; postwar economies were booming too. A powerful new demographic, teenagers, had financial and cultural influence, and they no longer wanted to dress like miniature versions of their parents. "There was a time when every girl under twenty yearned to look like an experienced, sophisticated thirty," fashion designer Mary Quant wrote in her autobiography. "All this is in reverse with a vengeance now. Suddenly every girl with a hope of getting away with it is aiming not only to look under voting age but under the age of consent."[1] Quant was the seminal purveyor of the "London Look." With its bright colors and inexpensive man-made materials, the London Look challenged the very idea of fashion, making it more individual, playful, and democratic than the couture sold across the English Channel. In April 1966, just as Quant was inventing hot pants, *Time* magazine dedicated an entire issue to her "Swinging City." Boutiques like Quant's Bazaar, Barbara Hulanicki's Biba, the Beatles' Apple Boutique, and Nigel Waymouth's Granny Takes a Trip catered to a young clientele more concerned with novelty (and affordability) than quality, prefiguring today's "fast fashion." As plastic flowers, cutouts, and Day-Glo microminis exploded from the streets of Chelsea to the Paris runways, the *New York Times* predicted: "Pop fashion, by that or any other name, is here to stay. Crazy stockings and hairdos, grossly synthetic fabrics, comic messages printed on dresses—these can be the ingredients of pop fashion. But, essentially, pop fashion is an irreverent attitude that bridles at solemnity about clothes."[2]

These new, youth-oriented styles ranged from playful to vulgar, depending on one's perspective, but their spirit of anarchy—mirroring the restless mood of the times—was impossible to ignore. While Seventh Avenue had once collectively dictated seasonal trends to a grateful nation, designers could no longer agree on so much as a standard hemline. Minis, midis, and maxis jostled for prominence on the White House runway. Trousers were creeping into women's wardrobes, though many designers hedged their bets by pairing them with long tunics or coats that doubled as dresses. Standards of beauty, prestige, and propriety were in flux. The show inadvertently highlighted that, both at the time and, even more so, in retrospect. As American society changed—and kept changing—so did the role and meaning of fashion in it.

Fashion and politics have always been a volatile combination, particularly for women, who cannot retreat into the sober anonymity of a suit and tie. It is as much a truism today as it was in 1968—or 1776, for that matter—that elected officials and their families must dress appropriately without appearing to spend taxpayers' money frivolously. George Washington set a presidential precedent of wearing American-made clothing, going to great lengths—Connecticut—to find a wool mill that could produce broadcloth of a quality comparable to that imported from Britain for his inaugural suit. But the burden of flying the fashion flag often fell to First Ladies; as Michelle Obama once quipped, nobody noticed that her husband wore the same tuxedo during his eight years in office, even as her wardrobe was minutely scrutinized. Dolley Madison and Mary Todd Lincoln are remembered for their extravagance; Lou Henry Hoover, Eleanor Roosevelt, and Bess Truman for their dowdiness. Mamie Eisenhower was unique for loving clothes while ignoring fashion. And American women basked in the reflected glory of Jacqueline Kennedy, a youthful, stylish First Lady who became an international trendsetter. But what these women with no formal platforms or portfolios had in common was that they selected their clothing out of patriotism as much as personal taste, believing that they were doing their duty to their country by dressing up—or down, as circumstances warranted. Indeed, through their wardrobe choices and patronage of homegrown designers, they were setting an example for their countrywomen of what it meant to be American.

The First Lady

It was not the famously chic First Lady Jacqueline Kennedy who brought Seventh Avenue to Pennsylvania Avenue but her middle-aged, middlebrow, middle-American successor, Claudia "Lady Bird" Johnson—a woman who never expected or aspired to become First Lady and who struggled to live up to the stylish example of her predecessor.

Raised a tomboy on a prosperous East Texas cotton plantation—"Lady Bird" was a childhood nickname—she attended the University of Texas, graduating in 1933 with a journalism degree. The following year, she married ambitious congressional aide Lyndon Baines Johnson after a whirlwind courtship. Thrust into politics when she married, she disliked crowds and making speeches. But Lady Bird Johnson was no "proud housewife," as the *Washington Post* had once described Mamie Eisenhower.[1] She was a shrewd and successful businesswoman, having parlayed a $67,000 inheritance into a million-dollar Austin broadcasting and real estate empire.[2] Indeed, she was the first First Lady to be a millionaire in her own right.

Though she was a Texan at heart, Johnson spent most of her adult life in Washington as her husband,

Claudia Alta "Lady Bird" Taylor as a child in East Texas. (LBJ Library photo by Unknown)

Lady Bird looks on as Lyndon takes the oath of office aboard Air Force One on November 22, 1963. (LBJ Library photo by Cecil Stoughton)

a Democrat, rose from aide to representative, from representative to senator, from senator to senate majority leader, and, finally, to vice president. When President John F. Kennedy was assassinated on November 22, 1963, she suddenly found herself in the national spotlight. On the plane home from Dallas that fateful day, moments after her husband had taken the oath of office on a borrowed Bible, Mrs. Johnson expressed her shock and anguish to Jacqueline Kennedy: "Oh, Mrs. Kennedy, you know we never even wanted to be Vice President and now, dear God, it's come to this."[3] For a woman who, it was said, "never jumps into anything," it was a rude awakening.[4] During her subsequent five years in the White House, she wrestled with the conviction that she was an illegitimate First Lady—not just in the country's eyes but in her own.

For years, the assassination hung like a dark cloud over the Johnson presidency, and Jackie Kennedy's legacy haunted Mrs. Johnson in ways both meaningful and mundane. As First Lady, she had to keep engagements made by Jackie, hang curtains and paintings purchased by Jackie, and endure being called "Mrs. Kennedy" in receiving lines. *Vogue* praised Mrs. Johnson for showing "respect for what can only fairly be described as her heavy inheritance," but the transition from Second Lady to First Lady was not an easy one.[5] She chronicled her private struggles in the oral diary she began keeping on the day of the assassination.

Although Mrs. Johnson had honed her public image as a congressional wife and on the presidential campaign trail—where she often stood in for

Jackie Kennedy, who was pregnant in the run-up to the 1960 election—she was a reluctant celebrity. "I have a sort of schizophrenic feeling that I'm cast in a role that I was never meant for," she admitted.[6]

She wasn't alone in that suspicion. The press took a decidedly skeptical attitude toward Johnson, mocking the Second Lady's plainspoken Texas twang, conservative hairstyle, and countrified manners, such as her insistence on driving her own car and traveling without a maid. Press photos of the Johnsons relaxing in jeans, boots, and cowboy hats on their Texas ranch did nothing to endear them to reporters enchanted by the preppy, patrician Kennedys. "She looked more like the ranch hand's wife than the ranch owner's," *Women's Wear Daily* quipped.[7] The "bible of fashion" famously crowned the First Lady "Her Elegance" while dubbing the Second Lady "Her Efficiency" and repeatedly accused Her Efficiency of having "Texas taste"—which was to say, no taste at all.

Johnson was complicit in cultivating her homespun, thrifty reputation. Before she set off on the campaign trail in 1960, the *Washington Post* noted that she'd acquired a "glamorous new wardrobe" at Neiman Marcus in Dallas. "We got some good values in their after-Christmas sale, but it wasn't an accident," Mrs. Johnson boasted to a reporter. "We went especially for the sale."[8] Even her most high-profile outfits made multiple appearances, not just at different events but on different Johnson women or female

Lady Bird and Lyndon on the LBJ Ranch near Stonewall, Texas, in 1959 (LBJ Library photo by Frank Muto)

Lady Bird on the LBJ Ranch in 1965 (LBJ Library photo by Yoichi Okamoto)

houseguests. She coaxed a long life out of a favorite, pricey beaded evening jacket by ordering a new dress to go under it every year. She rarely wore jewelry, and when she did, she stuck to the same trusty pearls and diamond bracelet she'd had for years.[9] Her mortified teenage daughters, Lynda Bird and Luci, had to beg her to buy new shoes, which she was reluctant to do until hers wore out completely.[10] Her husband frequently joked that she "would spend two hours trying to get something for two cents less."[11]

Much of the press coverage of the Second Lady's wardrobe consisted of damning with faint praise. Hope Miller, editor-in-chief of *Diplomat* magazine, diplomatically observed: "She is not a trend setter but buys good clothes and wears them for some time." *Women's Wear Daily*, which rose to national prominence thanks to its obsessive chronicling of Jacqueline Kennedy's wardrobe, treated Johnson with considerable skepticism. She "likes the no-fuss, no feathers look for both day and evening," *Women's Wear Daily* reported. She "prefers pretty feminine things to chic clothes and friends say her taste is sometimes fluffier than current fashions." A "cautious shopper," she "never buys on impulse, thinks carefully how each item will fit into her wardrobe, how it will clean, pack and travel. . . . Her favorite store is Neiman-Marcus and she has great faith in its executives who advise her."[12] The Dallas department store had been dressing Mrs. Johnson since her college days; the *New York Times* cited anonymous sources criticizing her "almost childlike dependence on the Texas concern" as evidence of her "lack of assurance in the fashion world."[13]

Stanley Marcus, the store's Harvard-educated president, seemed to confirm this when he recounted her first visit, shortly after her husband was elected to Congress in 1937. She "had no daringness and she had not too much self-confidence in her taste," he said. "She was always concerned whether she was going to look right and whether it was becoming." Of course, anything she purchased for herself had to be approved by her husband, who "exercised a very powerful veto," Marcus testified. "There were a lot of returns, but we learned pretty well what the guidelines were, and we tried not to violate them." LBJ "had very definite ideas of what he wanted the women around him to look like, and he had some antipathies to certain fashions that made it very difficult for us to serve him properly and at the same time dress the women properly," as Marcus delicately put it. "He didn't like full skirts; he didn't like tweeds."[14] In LBJ's opinion, thick, wooly textiles were "saddle blanket fabrics."[15] He hated what he called "muley" colors, like green, purple, brown, beige, and gray, preferring bright hues. Black was banned.[16] "He likes the things that show the shape of your figure, if you have one to show," Mrs. Johnson's social secretary, Bess Abell, noted in 1969.[17] "Unfortunately, fashion didn't always go along with him," Marcus pointed out.[18]

The young congressman took charge of his wife's wardrobe, telling her what to buy or, often, buying clothes for her without consulting her. (Marcus kept a dress form made to Mrs. Johnson's measurements, eliminating the need for fittings.)[19] "He does that not just with his wife," Abell revealed. "He does it with his daughters and he does it with his secretaries and he does it with anybody who will sit still and listen."[20] As senate majority leader, LBJ extended his largesse to his female secretaries and staffers, buying them gifts of clothing or sending them to Neiman Marcus, where his idiosyncratic tastes were well known. "The president was, in my opinion, sort of the last of the big Texas spenders," said Mollie Parnis, one of the First Lady's favorite designers.[21] He even encouraged his female employees to take time off to go to the hairdresser. "If they were going to be working all those long hours, he wanted them around to look good for him and look good for his visitors and not look frazzled and haggard," Abell explained.[22] LBJ insisted that his wife wear lipstick and take lessons from a makeup artist. "It matters to him how I look and he is proud that he thinks I do not look old, and that I have improved in grooming and looks and dress in the last ten years," Mrs. Johnson confided to her diary in 1967, adding: "I must have had a puritan ancestor because I always have a sort of a guilty silly feeling when I make a big production out of making up."[23]

Indeed, to Mrs. Johnson's mind, her husband's interest in clothes was a moral failing; she had been raised to value substance over style. "I had the idea that people were supposed to love me because I had an interesting mind, a kind heart, and a warm smile," she admitted. "I thought that

Lyndon's emphasis on clothes and appearance was the wrong system of values. He used to say that a lot of the people that I met would only see me once, and that the opinion they would form would persist. He wanted them to have a good opinion of me." She convinced herself that he was only looking out for her best interests. "By the world's rules, he was right. I was wrong."[24] As her diary indicates, she began paying more attention to fashion, carefully describing dresses she admired on other women.

Stanley Marcus took LBJ's fastidiousness with good-natured humor: "Every once in a while I would send a message back to him that if he would just pay as much attention to the affairs of the nation as he was to the skirt lengths and skirt widths of his women, that the country might be better off." After Kennedy's death, however, LBJ's micromanaging ceased. For once, he "just didn't have the time to take care of the affairs of the nation and the affairs of his feminine wardrobe," Marcus said.[25] Mrs. Johnson, long accustomed to having her clothes selected for her, found herself left to her own devices just as she was thrust into the national spotlight—a position at once liberating and terrifying.

Previously, Jackie had commanded the spotlight, and Lady Bird's fashion choices were of little concern to the media. But when she became First Lady, there was a surge of interest in her wardrobe from the press and the public alike. At first, the burden of her unexpected new duties prevented her from thinking about clothes at all—apart from the fact that she suddenly needed more of them, particularly eveningwear. Though LBJ hated black tie, Mrs. Johnson insisted on entertaining formally at the White House as often as possible: "I know it makes it a lot more special for the ladies, and for everybody really."[26] (By contrast, she rarely needed cocktail dresses—or "six o' clock dresses," as she called them.) Thus, in the chaotic early days of her husband's presidency, *Women's Wear Daily* reported that "a stream of White House aides is parading into [Washington, DC, department store] Garfinckel's these days to select outfits for Lady Bird Johnson."[27]

In a story headlined "The Eyes of Fashion Are upon Her," *Women's Wear Daily* interviewed friends, journalists, and fashion insiders—many of whom later attended the White House fashion show—for their opinions of the new First Lady. The replies were diplomatic, even complimentary. But many seemed to share the sentiments of Oleg Cassini, Kennedy's official designer, who found Mrs. Johnson "a charming person" who "dresses well" but added, "To me, Mrs. Kennedy is still the First Lady." The *New York Times* quoted "a long-time acquaintance" describing Mrs. Johnson as "tacky" when she arrived in Washington—a first impression that proved hard to overcome.[28] *Women's Wear Daily* charitably noted that her fashion sense had improved since her days as a congressional wife, undoubtedly shaped by her steady exposure to Washington society: "Now it's more classic and citified than Plain Old Texas." Dallas fashion industry veteran Christian Mann defended Mrs. Johnson's "innate good taste, even if at the moment it may appear provincial." But the fashion press still found opportunity to criticize her conservatism and frugality. "The Johnsons are a clothes-conscious family, but they don't spend big amounts of money," *Women's Wear Daily* reported.[29] If one reads between the lines, the portrait of a showy but unsophisticated Texan emerges. As they said in Dallas, the Johnsons were all hat, no cattle.

Stanley Marcus pushed back against this notion. "Mrs. Johnson's whole idea all her life was to dress neatly but not gaudily," he said. "Her dressing came slightly on the prosaic side, in large part because of what the President would let her wear and what he wouldn't let her wear." As First Lady, she dressed "in a classic fashion. Well, *Women's Wear* doesn't like classics. They like things that make news. If she had worn pants to the inauguration, they would have been delighted, because it would have been a news story."[30]

In May 1964, Mrs. Johnson participated in what was already a hallowed rite of passage for American First Ladies, a *Vogue* interview and photo shoot. Legendary lensman Horst P. Horst photographed her in the White House, wearing a sleeveless red evening sheath with a boat neck and a bow at the Empire waistline, paired with a pearl necklace—very much in the Jackie Kennedy mold. (*Vogue* neglected to credit the gown's designer; for a later Horst photo shoot in the White House gardens in 1967 she wore a forest green double-breasted coat and dress by Mollie Parnis.) The article praised her intelligence and dignity, describing her as "totally unlike the nation's folksy impression of her." Tellingly, the reporter felt it necessary to add: "She is definitely the First Lady."[31] Behind the scenes, however, the First Lady found the glamorous photo shoot a chore. "In the afternoon, I put in one of those long two hours getting dressed up in a red evening dress and going downstairs, first to the Red Room and where I do think it looks beautiful; and then into the Blue Room, posing for *Vogue* magazine," she recorded in her diary. "The picture will be in color—a cover picture perhaps—and it simply devours time." In the end, *Vogue* used the Blue Room picture, and it did not appear on the cover.[32]

Shortly after Mrs. Johnson moved into the White House, her long-time press secretary Liz Carpenter announced that—in a break with the Jaqueline Kennedy era—the White House would not release the names of the First Lady's designers or clothing stores, just descriptions of her outfits—"and we'll need help with that." (Carpenter, a brash Texan, "looks like a female Jonathan Winters and her timing and delivery in telling stories comes across almost as effectively," according *Women's Wear Daily*, her personal bête noire.)[33] Unlike most First Ladies, Mrs. Johnson had no time to prepare for her tenure; furthermore, there was barely a year left in Kennedy's unfinished term, which made long-term planning difficult. That fall, however, LBJ ran as the incumbent and won, badly beating Barry Goldwater. Mrs. Johnson remembered a "hilarious session" with Carpenter and Robin Duke, the stylish wife of the president's chief of protocol, "trying to describe each of my Inaugural costumes. . . . We might as well have been trying to write in Sanskrit. Neither Liz nor I knew the vocabulary of the clothing trade, or fashion designers. I hope I come out of this with dignity intact."[34]

The policy of secrecy may have begun as an attempt to avoid comparisons with Kennedy—whose wardrobe choices (and expenditures) the media had obsessively chronicled—but it also suited Mrs. Johnson, who

Lady Bird photographed in the Blue Room by Horst P. Horst for the May 1, 1964, issue of *Vogue* (Horst P. Horst, Condé Nast/ Shutterstock)

Red, White, and Blue on the Runway

Lady Bird and Liz Carpenter on the campaign trail in 1960 (LBJ Library photo by Frank Muto)

once confessed: "I never know what designer I am wearing if I don't look at the label."[35] The First Lady even took care to keep her designers unknown to each other, carefully scheduling fitting sessions so they would not meet in the halls.[36] Mrs. Johnson rarely mentioned who designed the outfits she described in her diary, identifying them by their details or by the occasion for which she originally purchased them; thus, "my Princess Margaret dress," "my See America dress," and "my wedding dress" (meaning her mother-of-the-bride dress). This did not keep the fashion press from speculating or from hounding those designers known to dress the First Family.

Mrs. Johnson was painfully aware of her sartorial inferiority to Mrs. Kennedy—"that immaculate woman," as she once called her.[37] Though Jackie was 17 years her junior, Mrs. Johnson idolized her, treating her with a reverential mix of starstruck awe and motherly protection. They first met as senators' wives. "I felt, as I expect a lot of us felt, like here is a bird of beautiful plumage among all of us little gray wrens," Johnson recalled.[38] Kennedy's perfection threw Johnson's deficiencies into high relief. "She always wore gloves like she was used to them," she reflected. "I never could."[39] While Jackie Kennedy made the pillbox hat her signature headwear—the press christened the ubiquitous style the "Jackie Box"—Mrs. Johnson preferred to go hatless; as far as she was concerned, the only reason to wear a hat was to hide a bad hair day. Privately, she referred to the pillbox as "the monkey hat—like you need an organ grinder to go with it."[40]

While Kennedy stunned in columnar floor-length evening gowns, Mrs. Johnson preferred "street-length" dresses for all but the most formal occasions. "A staircase in long dress and high heel shoes is always a mental hazard to me," she admitted.[41] She had a penchant for matchy-matchy ensembles of hat, dress, and shoes in the same hue, old-fashioned even by the standards of the early 1960s. Her stockings frequently sagged at the ankles.[42] Poignantly, when she inherited Mrs. Kennedy's "exquisite" White House dressing room "with the closets all covered with trompe l'oeil," Her Efficiency turned it into a makeshift office.[43]

But Johnson's conviction of the utter impossibility of living up to the example of Her Elegance may have been an advantage in the end. As Mollie Parnis pointed out, "It would be a big mistake if she tried to copy Mrs. Kennedy." Another designer who had dressed her, Roxane Kaminstein, noted, "Her influence will be different . . . she will appeal to a different type of person."[44] In other words, no-longer-young women of middle America finally had a First Lady to whom they could relate.

Jacqueline Kennedy was not the only fashion plate to impress and intimidate Mrs. Johnson. No prominent woman of the era could escape the soul-destroying influence of a unique form of social taxonomy: the International Best Dressed List. Beginning in 1940, pioneering New York fashion publicist Eleanor Lambert polled fashion editors across the country every December to compile a list of 10 women, announced in January. The list was usually drawn from high society and royalty but occasionally included heads of state, ambassadors' wives, media personalities, and Hollywood actresses (fashion industry professionals were ineligible). Lambert emphasized that the list was not meant to honor "great expenditure in clothes" but "people who know how to get it all together. . . . We tend to see personalities as symbols of their time. That's what the Best Dressed list aims to do."[45] Repeat winners could be promoted to the Best Dressed Hall of Fame, as Mrs. Kennedy was in 1965; this excluded them from the annual competition, allowing new nominees to take their place.

This brutally public, expert assessment of female fashionability was never far from Mrs. Johnson's mind. She described Evangeline Bell Bruce—the wife of the American ambassador to the United Kingdom—as "beautiful and young and on the best-dressed list always. This always makes me feel quite small." At a party in New York two weeks before the White House fashion show, she caught a glimpse of the stylish 24-year-old socialite Amanda Burden, Babe Paley's daughter: "She's the youngest woman to have ever made the best dressed list. And I, like every other woman in the room, took in carefully the covered up white elegance and the simplicity of her dress." When a newspaper cruelly claimed "that the First Lady never would compete with the best dressed," it was not a casual insult; it referenced a specific, identifiable group of women, with all the privilege, breeding, and fame they represented.[46]

Along with Mrs. Kennedy, Mrs. Johnson spoke reverentially of Queen Sirikit of Thailand, Balmain's best customer. "Every time I see her I remember that I have read she is one of the world's best dressed women," she recorded in her diary. "It is a flag that sort of precedes you once you have got the title." Of the stunning Empress Farah Diba of Iran, who visited the White House in 1967, she mused: "When a visiting chief of state has a wife as beautiful as she is, there is that hushed moment of excitement after he's gotten out when you wait for her to emerge from the big black car, eager to see what she is wearing, how she has her hair done, what jewels. She is an ornament to her husband and to her country as is the Queen of

When the Johnsons dined with King Bhumibol and Queen Sirikit of Thailand at Bangkok's Grand Palace during their 1966 "Asian Odyssey," Mrs. Johnson wore a George Stavropoulos chiffon gown and the queen wore a formal Thai Boromphiman, which Lady Bird described in her diary in clinical detail: "ruby red, high neck, long sleeves, girdled with gold with an enormous gold ornament in the front and lovely chandelierlike Thai earrings." (Bettmann/Getty Images)

Thailand—perhaps the two outstanding ones I have met."[47] The First Lady appreciated that a political wife's wardrobe could be a powerful instrument of diplomacy.

But that didn't mean she had to enjoy fashion. Indeed, her antipathy to it was such that she limited her shopping excursions to twice a year, to shop the spring and fall collections. "In this life, there are at least two days, maybe more, in about February, and about August, that are devoted entirely to clothes," she recorded in her diary.[48] The Carlyle Hotel in New York kept a 34th-floor apartment reserved for the First Family; the Trumans had stayed there, and the Kennedys used it so often that it became known as "the New York White House." It was there that Mrs. Johnson carried out the distasteful business of trying on, buying, and being fitted for her clothes.

Accompanied by Bess Abell and sometimes her daughters or close friends, the First Lady holed up in her suite while a parade of designers and models came and went bearing samples, sketches, and fabric swatches. Occasionally she ventured outdoors, buying shoes (size 8AAA) from Delman's or Bergdorf Goodman. "You can't send your feet out to get fitted for shoes," she lamented. Similarly, she went to Adolfo for her hats (a marked upgrade from her pre–White House milliner, Miss Ceil of Jacque-Lynn in Washington) and picked up other necessities at Lord and Taylor.[49] "Ever efficient Mrs. Lyndon Johnson goes shopping with a garment diary tucked into her handbag," the Associated Press reported. "The diary containing fabric swatches of the clothes she already owns aids her in picking compatible colors and textures."[50] Before LBJ ran for reelection in 1964, she spent an entire day ensconced at the Carlyle, trying on racks of garments from Neiman Marcus, Adele Simpson, Bill Blass, and Norman Norell, who arrived with a maid and fitters in tow. "A campaign is rather like an iceberg," she remarked. "There is so much below the surface that doesn't show. And part of the work is getting clothes assembled." After another fitting session, in 1967, she mused: "How funny that just trying on clothes should be so tiring."[51]

The only benefit to these torture sessions was that once they were over, Mrs. Johnson could take her mind off clothes completely for months at a time. Each shopping trip concluded with a similar statement. "Soon I hope I'll get this all wrapped up and never have to think about it again until summer," she remarked in January 1964. A few days later: "I . . . am going to buy one or two and hope I can soon get clothes out of my life for the next three or four months." The next day: "I look forward to the time right soon when I'll be through with clothes." And, the following year: "I hope I'll get enough clothes in these years never to have to go back again!"[52]

Just as she had relied on Stanley Marcus and his staff in Dallas, Mrs. Johnson now sought fashion advice from a small group of trusted designers, as well as a tight-knit circle of supporters in Washington and New York. "Mrs. Johnson is a great advice-seeker," Liz Carpenter said of her approach to dressing.[53] She had in-person fittings with Mollie Parnis, Adele Simpson, and George Stavropoulos, Seventh Avenue designers who were well known for their feminine, flattering clothing without being in the upper echelons of style—or price. (Naturally, all of the Johnson women patronized American designers exclusively.) Clara Treyz, a retired "merchandise counselor" for Neiman Marcus, acted as a personal shopper and a go-between with designers represented by the store, like Simpson and Marquise.[54] Mildred Custin, the president of Bonwit Teller, was her link to Stavropoulos and Ben Zuckerman. "And most of all Bess—resourceful, tactful, reminding, threading it all together. And in the background, Helen [Williams, her maid], whom I always think is looking at me rather disapprovingly because I don't get enough."[55]

And then there was Robin Duke, the glamorous fourth wife of Angier Biddle Duke, President Kennedy's chief of protocol, who stayed on for a year after the assassination to ease the transition for the Johnsons.[56] A former model and fashion editor, Duke would make the International Best Dressed List in 1966. (She went on to become an ambassador, philanthropist, and activist.) "Robin is probably my best authority in the world of fashion, if I were to try to really learn about that world, which I'm not," Mrs. Johnson insisted. She "knows so much about it, dresses so well, is so sure in her touch."[57]

It was Duke who advised Mrs. Johnson on how to transform the many exotic textiles she received as gifts or brought home as souvenirs from foreign trips—like a sari presented to her by Indira Gandhi—into suits and gowns she could wear in her role as First Lady. She introduced the First Lady to her personal dressmaker, "the dapper little Japanese" Kandi Ohno, and newcomer John Moore, the Texan who made Mrs. Johnson's gown for the 1965 inaugural ball. Duke even accompanied Mrs. Johnson on some of her New York shopping trips, though it was an ordeal for both of them. "I keep on suppressing a desire to giggle, and I have the feeling I'm going back to being *me* very shortly. But at least it's a new world to learn, and Robin is so knowledgeable, sharp and kindly about it, although I think her patience even is threadbare at this point."[58]

It is due to, not despite, Mrs. Johnson's skeptical attitude toward fashion that her diary is such a vivid and valuable record of the unique requirements

The First Lady called former model and fashion editor Robin Chandler Duke—wearing an Adolfo hat in Chicago in 1967—"my best authority in the world of fashion." (*Chicago Daily News*)

and mechanics of the First Lady's wardrobe. "You stand and stand and look at swatches and make lists of last year's things and what you need to fit in for the big events of the year that require new dresses—the Congressional brunch, the Senate ladies lunch, the diplomatic reception, a long party dress for the military reception, and of course arrival ceremony clothes." Often, several such events took place in quick succession. "Sometimes living in the White House means a ridiculous number of changes per day, one for each occasion," she noted in her diary. She disliked wearing gowns with trains, because they got trampled in crowds and made it difficult to dance. (Dancing with her 6'4" husband brought its own challenges; it "sort of pulls you up," Mrs. Johnson explained after one White House reception, "which I am afraid gives a noticeable effect on my dress, which is already daringly short.") Far from being a pampered lady of leisure, she often had to get dressed in a hurry or in less-than-ideal conditions. "You have to be careful to choose which evening dress, the simplest one, when you're changing in a lurching airplane, and transferring to a helicopter." On one shopping trip, she told Liz Carpenter: "This is a good tree-planting dress."[59]

Skirts had to be "short enough to be stylish, but long enough so she doesn't feel uncomfortable sitting down," Carpenter explained.[60] Bess Abell remembered that during fittings Mrs. Johnson "would always move a chair over in front of the mirror and sit down and see if she could sit down and not need to reach for a scarf or a program or an enormous handbag to cover her knees."[61] She liked silk and wool knits for traveling, "because they're so packable."[62] (Even as First Lady, she refused to travel with a maid.) Many of her dresses had matching coats or jackets, so she could look polished in any weather. On her shopping trips to New York, she found herself "remembering what were my favorite things of the past season, what looked best in pictures, what survived the long days freshest, and what holds the day's problems, what was absolutely impossible to sit on the platform in."[63]

While she had a marked preference for feminine, flowing chiffons, her wardrobe choices were dictated by political expediency, not personal taste. As her predecessor in the role of Second Lady, Pat Nixon, once told the *New York Times:* "I never buy a dress just because I like it. I think, will it pack? Is it conservative enough?"[64] Mrs. Johnson proclaimed to *Women's Wear Daily:* "Clothes have to serve me, not I serve the clothes."[65] And they served her diligently. "Rarely ever did she buy anything, as most women do, that just hung in her closet," Abell said.[66]

Like many in her position, Mrs. Johnson took care to wear special pieces for special occasions, considering the color of the room, the makeup of the guest list, the possibility of wearing diplomatic gifts, the photo opportunities, and the theme of the event, such as choosing flower-trimmed dresses to support her beautification campaign or yellow when in Texas. In her diary, she recorded the mental gymnastics she performed while dressing for one typical White House event, a dinner for Japanese prime minister Eisaku Sato in 1967: "I went through that foolish feminine rigmarole about what to wear. Mollie Parnis was coming. I'd love to wear one of her dresses. And with Mr. Sato, the guest of honor, I just must wear my pearls that he had given me on the last trip. And then remembered that educational TV was doing a show on it. So it must photograph well. It couldn't be anything that I had worn lately. I finally wore my Adele Simpson gold chiffon and hoped for the best." For another official engagement, she reflected: "Choosing a dress for a day such as this is an important part of the planning."[67]

The oral history Bess Abell recorded for the Johnson Presidential Library in 1969 contains the following supremely condescending exchange with the (male) interviewer, T. H. Baker:

> BAKER: Some day in the future a lady scholar may be reading this and fault me if I don't ask you. What about such things as wardrobe, personal requirements like that?
>
> ABELL: That's something that you learn from your first trip too, because you realize that you don't want to ask a man "what do I wear," because they always say, "hat and white gloves." Sometimes you don't always need a hat and white gloves. Mrs. Johnson, as I'm sure you're aware, is terribly conscious of all details, and clothing falls under that umbrella as well. She would always try before she left on one of these trips, whether it was four days or three days in the Redwoods, or three weeks in Asia, to write down black dress, with yellow jacket by that; time to change—such-and-such; hair comb; evening dress—pink floral; shampoo and set. She would have a space on that schedule that she would have pencilled in what she was going to wear, and when she could have her hair combed; and the time in there when she thought she'd need, and have time for, a shampoo and set.
>
> BAKER: That's impressive.
>
> ABELL: It is impressive. There are a lot of lessons you can learn from that lady.
>
> BAKER: I could pass them on to my wife.[68]

Abell's testimony offers revealing insights into the First Lady's pragmatic, dispassionate approach to dressing for the job.

In her own oral history, Mollie Parnis—who had dressed Bess Truman and Mamie Eisenhower as well as Mrs. Johnson—listed some of the challenges of dressing First Ladies:

First of all, they don't buy many prints. The reason they don't buy many prints is that they're constantly photographed, and a print is too noticeable. They have to be sure that a dress "sits" gracefully. Their requirements are different than the average lady who is just buying her spring wardrobe or fall wardrobe. A minimum amount of detail on a dress means that when it's photographed more than once it isn't obvious. Then of course they have to do so many more functions. . . . It was nothing for the White House to have six important events a week, both luncheons and dinners. . . . The First Lady needs more evening clothes than other women. She needs large assortments of clothes for trips, it depends on where they are going. If they are campaigning, she needs clothes to campaign in. If they go on state visits, they need clothes that travel well. Oh, they need many, many more clothes than the average woman.

Parnis's only criticism of Mrs. Johnson's clothes when she entered the White House was "that she didn't have enough of them."[69] Alas, the sheer volume of clothing needed for the job was something the First Lady, with her aversion to spending money frivolously, never quite appreciated. "I never have the nerve to buy enough clothes at once," she admitted. "It always sounds like so much money. Helen looks at me in a wry way with a touch of almost disdain. And patient Bess encourages me and reminds me that there will be the so-and-so party and that reception and the other State Dinner." Preparing for one of her first major visits from a foreign dignitary—the Chanel-clad Queen of Greece, in 1964—Mrs. Johnson had a horrifying epiphany: "It begins to dawn on me that I *really* don't have any new clothes." It fell to Abell to cajole Mrs. Johnson into spending more, assuring her, "I will indeed need everything that I am getting and several more in addition I saw that I cannot afford." As punishment for her parsimoniousness, she was constantly forced to augment her dreaded twice-yearly New York shopping trips with "fill-in" sessions at the White House, and she often found her wardrobe coming up short at the last minute. She once bought a peach brocade Mollie Parnis dress and coat that she ended up wearing to an event that very evening, after Parnis hastily shortened the ensemble and lent her matching shoes and a purse.[70]

Her one indulgence was her hairdresser, Jean Louis, who coiffed her "in a room specially decorated in one of her favorite colors, pale blue." As designer Donald Brooks said of the First Lady: "Regardless of her type or way of dressing, her make-up and her hair styles have always been immaculate."[71] With the decline of hats, hair itself had become an important accessory.[72] Like many women of her time—including her daughters—Mrs. Johnson employed hairpieces, falls, and "postiches" (wiglets) to achieve the fashionable bouffant look, though she was extremely anxious to keep this beauty secret from the press. ("I am sure that I shall always look like a Russian in a big fur hat when I try to wear them.") She also relied on that mainstay of midcentury female fashion, the girdle, which was less of a minimizer than a stabilizer. Even thin women wore them.[73]

Bess Abell remembers telling Mrs. Johnson early on in her White House days: "I think it's wonderful that you buy things from Neiman's—the things everything else is wearing—but I don't want you to buy evening clothes in the same way. I think your evening clothes should be something different." The First Lady replied: "Bess that's just not important." Abell countered: "I know it's not important, but say that you and two of your honored guests arrive in the same costume! That, of course, will always become the story of the dinner, and that's not a compliment to your honored guests." Abell lamented: "I don't think it ever really sunk in."[74]

But one night, it finally did. "She was planning to wear a lovely green dress with a gold-embroidered jacket," Abell remembered. "I was downstairs as the guests were coming in and her dress walked in on Kay Graham—Mrs. Philip Graham of the *Washington Post*—I ran upstairs and said, 'You may want to change.' . . . I always felt that some guest who had really knocked themselves out getting this pretty dress to wear to the White House dinner didn't want to walk in and see the hired help wearing the same dress."[75] On another occasion, Mrs. Johnson arrived at a dinner party to find that the hostess—the "always magnificently dressed" Jane Englehard—was wearing the same gown in a different color. "As I stepped off the elevator, a cavern yawned before me," she shuddered at the memory. And she was miffed when the press reported that she had worn the same gown as Edward "Ted" Kennedy's wife to a Friends of the Kennedy Center benefit, though she had not.[76] Chastened, Mrs. Johnson began to have her eveningwear customized.[77] "The biggest sin seems to be to have the same dress as somebody else and to show up at the same party in it," she observed.[78]

Affairs of state could overtake her best-laid fashion plans. In 1968, Mrs. Johnson was having her hair dressed for a Democratic fundraising dinner when the awful news came that Dr. Martin Luther King Jr. had been assassinated. "Everybody's mind began racing off it its own direction as to what this would mean to racial violence in our country, to the work of so many to try to bring us together—how far would it throw us back. There I was with an elaborate hairdo, in Mr. Stavropolous's [sic] elegant, festive, flame-colored chiffon, ready for the Democratic dinner, which was already in progress. But the hands of the clock had stopped."[79] She took off her gown and spent a somber evening watching the news instead.

Above all, the First Lady's wardrobe had to stand up to intense scrutiny, from the press and public alike. "All of the people from whom we buy our clothes or get services—from Earle Williams, Lyndon's shirt man, to Jean

Louis, are being sought out and put under the microscope like insects on the point of a pin," Mrs. Johnson noted on the eve of the 1965 inauguration. "I don't blame them for not knowing what to do or say, but how I do love the anonymous ones who escape. So far, Mr. Per [her longtime hairdresser] has and there are quite a few purchases of gowns that I never heard of, all slightly annoying and trivial." Among Mollie Parnis's other qualifications, Mrs. Johnson appreciated her discretion. "Mollie sometimes tells interesting little anecdotes of her days with helping Mrs. Eisenhower. And I am always reassured and pleased that none of them would I mind being told if I were Mrs. Eisenhower." Given the press's frequently vicious nature, Mrs. Johnson confessed: "There are times when I think it is worth it to stay just a mouse, in the world of fashion."[80]

Yet her tastes grew more adventurous over the years. As she "became more independent, more on her own in the decisions, and more exposed to the clothes that women of position and wealth wore, we could see her beginning to swing over to some of the clothes that she had turned down in our store in previous years," Marcus reflected.[81] In her own way, she

Robin Duke introduced Lady Bird to fellow Texan John Moore, who made her "elegant, regal" coat and gown of sable and yellow satin for the 1965 inaugural ball. (LBJ Library photos by Unknown)

was as difficult a customer as her husband. She preferred off-the-rack, ready-to-wear clothes not just for their lower price but because she didn't like to shop from sketches and swatches; she wanted to see and feel the finished garment. On the few occasions she had things custom-made—like Moore's sable-cuffed coat and matching inaugural gown of yellow-rose-of-Texas satin—she worried that the final result would be disappointing. "I'm just not the type for sketches and swatches," she admitted. "I'm a go-in-and-look-on-the-rack, put-them-on-and-wear-them-out type."[82] She wasn't a sample size, though, so the finished garment was not always readily available. At 5'4" she was a size 8 with a 20-inch waist, according to the breathless reports of the fashion press—though privately she confessed to being a size 10, roughly equivalent to a size 4 in modern sizing.[83] "She's a hamburger girl who dieted from a 14 to a size 10," Adele Simpson told the Associated Press.[84] She also swam laps in the White House pool to keep her figure.[85]

Mrs. Johnson did not hesitate to wear the same dress twice, or more; even her inaugural ball ensemble withstood multiple wearings. She paired the fur-trimmed coat with a dress made from gold brocade gifted by Pakistani president Ayub Khan for a St. Patrick's Day exhibition opening at the National Gallery of Art in 1966; the next morning, the coat was flown to Hollywood, where Lynda wore it to a cocktail party that night.[86] Yet she never accepted discounts, rejecting high-end designers like James Galanos as too pricey. "She came in with the amount that she was going to spend on a given trip, and, believe me, she didn't go over it ten cents!" Marcus exclaimed.[87]

In 1966, her daughter Luci's upcoming wedding required Mrs. Johnson to take another trip to the Carlyle. Because of the intense public interest in the nuptials—the first White House wedding in more than 60 years—the hotel became "a sort of embattled fortress with the press stationed downstairs at every entrance in force, with plenty of cameras and recording such world-shaking news as that 'the well-known gown firm of Priscilla's of Boston slipped some entries into the suite on two hangers covered with muslin.' . . . One story began with, 'If official comment offers any key, the President's daughter will wear ankle-length secrecy under a short veil of "no comment."'" As Luci and her bridesmaids tried on gowns in a neighboring suite, Mrs. Johnson welcomed Mollie Parnis, Adele Simpson, and Clara Treyz of Neiman Marcus, eventually settling on a "lovely" yellow mother-of-the-bride dress and matching coat by Simpson. In her diary, she echoed the language of the Vietnam conflict: "I spent the morning in a big push on 'Operation Trousseau.'"[88]

Letters preserved in the Johnson Presidential Library reveal that even though the fashion press may have considered Mrs. Johnson overly cautious and conservative in her clothing choices, members of the public still found things to criticize, and their criticisms had to be answered. In particular, short skirts and sleeveless dresses drew complaints, often with newspaper clippings picturing the offending garment enclosed. "During the Democratic Convention you wore a sleeveless dress," Dorothea Anderson of Springfield, Illinois, wrote in 1964. "On the platform you waved to the crowd several times. The flesh on your upper arm swung back and forth as

Luci Johnson dressed for her 1966 wedding in the Lincoln Bedroom, where the models would later have their fittings for the fashion show. (Lyndon B. Johnson Presidential Library and Museum/NARA)

you waved like a bowl full of jelly. A dress with elbow length sleeves would eliminate this." Another concerned citizen wrote: "You are not teenager and you have ugly knees. Mrs. Kennedy could get could get away with it but not you, a Grandmother who should have some pride in herself. Your taste in clothes is disgusting. . . . But I guess you Johnsons just must stay in style—no matter how silly you look."[89] One writer entreated the First Lady and her daughters to wear more hats.[90] Occasionally, people asked where she had bought a particular dress or requested the donation of an outfit to a museum or fundraiser. Bess Abell penned a supremely diplomatic reply to a correspondent who complained about a too-high hemline: "Constructive criticism is difficult to convey. You have achieved it in a most dignified manner."[91] To a South Carolina couple, Abell added: "She is aware of her influence on fashion as the wife of the President, and for that reason is always conscious of her style of dress."[92]

However "annoying and trivial" fashion might be, Mrs. Johnson realized that she could not ignore it, and the fashion press held out hope that the First Lady might someday even learn to enjoy it. If her personal taste tended toward practicality and frugality, the demands of her position required an extensive and eye-catching wardrobe. "Mrs. Johnson is today more interested in fulfilling her important role in life than in just being a clothes horse," reported *Women's Wear Daily*. "But when she can project a tasteful and exciting fashion image at the same time . . . so much the better."[93]

As First Lady, Mrs. Johnson had several opportunities to develop an appreciation of fashion—not just its superficial appeal but its political and economic importance. The International Ladies' Garment Workers' Union was a powerful lobbying force in Washington, as Mrs. Johnson discovered when Luci inadvertently chose a wedding gown from a non-union manufacturer; the president had to intervene to avoid a scandal. "The world of clothes is quite an important one, I am finding out," Mrs. Johnson remarked after attending a dinner dance in New York in the company of Mollie Parnis, Eleanor Lambert, and *Vogue* editor Diana Vreeland. It was also an enjoyable one, as the First Lady could not help noticing. "I can't get over the slightly ridiculous feeling that clothes should take up so much time," she admitted. "And on the other hand, a sort of vain, feminine, increasing delight and thinking I look rather well in them, a bit younger and slimmer than a good many of my contemporaries."[94]

With the support of her husband and advisors, her sartorial stock continued to rise. *Women's Wear Daily* praised the "delightfully adventuresome" clothes Adele Simpson conjured up for the First Lady in the spring of 1966, which marked a departure from her usual wardrobe of "tired, safe classics" and took her "beyond the banal to a new fashion level." Nevertheless, she continued to buy from other designers "those standard, workaday clothes that fill out every woman's wardrobe. They are not exciting . . . but they are practical."[95]

The breakthrough came at the tail end of 1966. "There had been the most amazing news on the ticker," Johnson recorded in her diary. "In the list of best dressed women I showed up in fifth place along with two Fords and two Vanderbilts—Princess Lee Radziwill leading the list. Mollie Parnis or Adele Simpson or Stanley Marcus must have tried hard, but I don't deserve it." She suspected Eleanor Lambert—a presidential appointee to the National Council on the Arts—may have had a hand in her selection; her fashion mentor, Robin Duke, had made the list as well, along with Lauren Bacall and Sophia Loren. "And I shall strive a bit to live up to it. . . . I have no illusions. . . . I don't belong there."[96]

Her tenure on the best dressed list did not last long; the following year, she was replaced by her eldest daughter, Lynda—who deserved it more, she

Charles Robb, Lynda Johnson, Mrs. Johnson (wearing Mollie Parnis), and Luci and Patrick Nugent with Yuki, the family dog, on the LBJ Ranch in 1967 (LBJ Library photo by Yoichi Okamoto)

Red, White, and Blue on the Runway

felt. But the distinction gave her confidence, and it encouraged her to take pride and pleasure in her wardrobe. She even started to show an interest in jewelry. In 1967, she confessed somewhat guiltily: "I am almost bowing these days to the fashion dictate of a new dress for every great occasion." She was conforming to fashion in other ways, as well: "Luci's urging, Helen's silent disapproval, Mollie Parnis's politely qualified hopes, have finally driven me to raise my dresses another inch or so." And, a month later: "Shorter and shorter they go, and more accustomed does the eye become, and I am doing what I swore I never would—actually wearing them a little above the knees."[97] The press alternately blamed and praised Lynda and Luci for their mother's style apotheosis: "With the blossoming of her two daughters . . . Mrs. Johnson has become more youthful looking and au courant too."[98]

The First Lady finally admitted that she was "spoiled. It's a real joy to have clothes made especially for me that fit just right by people who care. Well, at any rate, I shall enjoy every day of it until we walk out of this office, and then not expect them to do it anymore."[99]

2

The Committee

Long before Mrs. Johnson made a surprise appearance on the International Best Dressed List, the idea of showcasing American fashion in the White House was hatched by two of the First Lady's most fashionable friends, Bess Abell and broadcaster Nancy Dickerson. "A handsome young brunette with big brown eyes and a honey voice," Dickerson was the first female CBS news correspondent and a longtime Johnson family friend; the Johnsons had owned a CBS affiliate in Dallas.[1] She was also a perennial nominee for the Best Dressed List. Eleanor Lambert even devoted one of her syndicated fashion columns to singing Dickerson's praises.[2] When, in 1966, Mrs. Johnson visited Big Bend, a little-known National Park in her home state, Dickerson accompanied the press pool. Despite the rustic locale—the First Lady referred to it as "roll-your-own country"—Dickerson "always managed to look like she just stepped out of *Vogue*," Mrs. Johnson marveled, adding: "And I'll assure you that the conditions were adverse." The delegation members even had to bring their own toilets.[3]

Publicity photo of NBC News correspondent Nancy Dickerson in 1970 (Wikimedia Commons)

In the hectic days following the assassination, Dickerson—by then working for NBC in Washington—acted as a fashion mentor to the entire Johnson family, lending Mrs. Johnson black coats and dresses from her own well-stocked closet and taking her "recalcitrant" teenage daughters shopping for clothes appropriate to their new public role.[4] As Dickerson's son remembered, "the First Lady, who was both rich and frugal, was astonished that anyone would have so many black clothes. Mom was shocked that Lady Bird didn't have any."[5] Of course, black was one of the colors LBJ had banned from his wife's wardrobe.

Dickerson was especially helpful when it came to advising Mrs. Johnson on what to wear for television appearances.[6] Though Dickerson was nearly as close in age to the Johnson daughters as to the First Lady herself, Mrs. Johnson saw her as a role model. "To me she is the very prototype of a

Bess Abell in the Red Room of the White House in October 1968, dressed for a party for the president of the Republic of Chad (LBJ Library photo by Robert Knudsen)

successful career woman who also majors in family life and social life," Mrs. Johnson reflected.[7] *Vogue* noted, admiringly, that Dickerson had once written a speech while under the hair dryer at Kenneth, the tony New York salon.[8]

Dickerson was not alone in trying to persuade Mrs. Johnson to show more interest in fashion, which the First Lady dismissed as "froufrou."[9] Abell embraced fashion as vigorously as the First Lady shunned it, often appearing on the boards of charity fashion shows and in the fashion press. Abell was Washington royalty in her own right. Her father, Earle C. Clements, had been governor of Kentucky and later a senator. Her stepfather-in-law, Drew Pearson, wrote the syndicated Washington Merry-Go-Round column. Both men were Johnson family friends. The young mother of two lent the Johnson White House some Jackie-esque glamour. In 1961, *Women's Wear Daily* reported on a surprise birthday party the "pert, pretty" social secretary to the then Second Lady threw for her husband, Tyler; her "dome-skirted chocolate and white print polished cotton" dress was the "perfect foil for her honey-blond artichoke hairdo."[10] (Tyler Abell would replace Angier Biddle Duke as LBJ's chief of protocol in 1968.) As the First Lady's social secretary, shopping companion, and resident style expert, Abell was perfectly placed to convince Mrs. Johnson that a fashion show—and fashion in general—was a good idea.

Though there was no precedent for hosting a fashion show in the White House, there was ample precedent for doing so almost anywhere else. In the 1950s and '60s, fashion shows—or "style shows," as Mrs. Johnson called them—were "a tribal ritual," she once explained. "Every ladies' luncheon or every ladies' benefit of any sort was likely to have a style show hooked onto it, ladies parading down the walkway in fancy clothes. Hats, hats, hats. Gloves. One thought a lot about clothes in those days."[11]

Looking back years later, Mrs. Johnson struggled to explain why women of her generation devoted so much time to dressing and socializing, instead of charity work or public service. "We had made such a strenuous effort from December 7, 1941, to the end of the war and on for several years. We'd done without so much; we'd worked so hard. We'd been so determined to win that we were happy to relax and just live it up." Luncheons, teas, and style shows "were part of the pattern of life." Mrs. Johnson confessed: "We could spend three hours in the middle of the day doing that." As a congressional wife, she had attended many such events in Washington, and found them refreshingly bipartisan. "Politics stopped at the door," she remembered. "You'd be sitting by somebody whose husband you knew was pretty much a mortal enemy of your husband, but we never let it bother us."[12]

The invitations to fashion shows that Mrs. Johnson and her daughters received—and invariably declined—fill a two-inch-thick file in the Lyndon B. Johnson Library. They came from a bewildering variety of far-flung organizations, including the Naval Officer's Wives Club; the Potomac Chapter of the National Society of Interior Designers; the Darlington Parent Teacher Association of Harford County, Maryland; the Texas Colorado Lakes Council of Girl Scouts; the Faculty Wives of Glassboro State College; and the Women's Auxiliary of the American Dental Association.[13] Regardless of her feelings about "froufrou," the First Lady was simply too busy to accept every invitation she received, and she could not accept one without offending someone else. Along with her regrets, she routinely offered fashion show organizers framed, signed photos of the White House to use as door prizes—continuing a Kennedy tradition. In a few cases, if the charity was politically sensitive or close to her heart, she agreed to act as the patron of a fashion show without actually attending it. In April 1962, Mrs. Johnson—then Second Lady—served as honorary chairman of the National Democratic Club fashion lunch, at which Pauline Trigère presented her summer collection. Several travel costumes illustrated the show's theme, "Holiday U.S.A."[14]

One of the rare fashion shows the First Lady did attend took place in a venue even stranger than the White House: an American Airlines jet en route from Washington to San Francisco. On September 20, 1966, Mrs. Johnson embarked on a four-day "Faces of the West" tour of California, Arizona, and New Mexico. She traveled on a chartered 727 filled with journalists, aides, and secret servicemen, plus Secretary of the Interior Stewart Udall and his wife, Lee. It was "as remarkable a flight as any American Airlines Jet ever had," Mrs. Johnson remembered. "Including some 63 passengers, press, photographers, Cyril Magnin, fashion models, 40 different outfits for them to wear, Secret Service, staff and me,

The First Lady enjoys a fashion show aboard a chartered American Airlines 727 en route to San Francisco in 1966. (LBJ Library, White House Naval Photographic Unit, Outs Roll 2 of 2 from MP1039, *Faces of the West*)

and my seedling from the White House Lawn. All we lacked was a beagle." Fifteen minutes after takeoff, cocktails were served and the fashion show began, "the girls changing in a space the size of a telephone booth." The clothes were "pure California, ranging from vinyl sheaths, mini skirts, and earrings as big as golf balls, and pant suits and metallic gold stockings. . . . There were lots for Lynda Bird and Luci to love, but not for me."[15]

But the entire show was produced for an audience of one: the First Lady. Titled "What the Well-Dressed Woman Doer and Traveler Wears When Discovering America," it was organized by Joseph Magnin, the West Coast department store "catering to the bright young woman."[16] The store's director, its namesake's son Cyril I. Magnin, was a friend of President Johnson's and a member of the President's Committee for Equal Opportunity in Housing. (He had also been married to Adele Simpson's sister Anna Smithline—a successful designer in her own right—until her death in 1948.) The *Washington Post* described the clothes as being suitable for "planting trees, making speeches or taking beautification tours. Leisure and evening wear will also be shown on the flight"—consciously mirroring Mrs. Johnson's own wardrobe needs.[17] One evening gown was even called the Yellow Rose of Texas.[18]

Newsreel footage shows Mrs. Johnson seated next to Lee Udall, with Magnin and the secretary behind them, as models in hats, white gloves, and false eyelashes parade up and down the narrow aisle. (One carries a copy of the president's book, *My Hope for America*.) At one point, a model pauses in front of the First Lady and opens her white jacket for a big reveal: a red, white, and blue striped top. Mrs. Johnson laughs and claps her hands in obvious delight.[19] In her diary, she admitted that she'd been impressed by "a few well tailored gray suits, and a smashing red, white and blue outfit by Bill Blass that I would like to have had."[20] She later remarked: "I have rarely so enjoyed a flight."[21] It was a memorable event for Cyril Magnin too. A year later, Joseph Magnin was enlisted to supply Lynda Bird Johnson's trousseau when she married Capt. Charles Robb—a coup for the store that had long been regarded as a down-market alternative to its tony hometown rival, I. Magnin, founded by Cyril's grandmother.

Given the ubiquity of fashion shows in 1960s political and charitable circles, it's surprising that a White House fashion show didn't happen sooner. The idea seems to have been hatched fairly early on in the Johnson administration, shortly after the January 1965 inauguration. It was first mentioned in a letter from Bess Abell to Eleanor Lambert dated April 15, 1965. "When you return [from Japan] I would like very much to explore an idea with you—one which I believe you and Nancy Dickerson have discussed briefly," Abell wrote. "Could you please telephone me at the White House?"[22]

If Lambert replied, nothing came of it right away. Of course, she was a busy woman. In 1939, the newly formed New York Dress Institute, backed by labor unions and clothing manufacturers, had hired Lambert—publicist to both Adele Simpson and Mollie Parnis—as its press director. Her mission was to promote American fashion at a time when the once-dominant French industry was crippled by World War II. In 1943, Lambert launched the biannual media feeding frenzy we now know as New York Fashion Week, originally called Press Week. "The American garment industry is now in a position to prove whether it can make a silk dress, or whether it will be a sow's ear," quipped Stanley Marcus.[23]

Press Week had a transformative effect on both the internal and external perception of the American fashion industry. It was the first of the "Big Four" fashion weeks; Milan did not follow suit until 1958, trailed by Paris in 1973 and London in 1984. And it was instrumental in establishing the supremacy of Seventh Avenue designers over the manufacturers who employed them. While Lambert did not hesitate to exploit consumers' wartime fervor to buy American, she recognized that personalities, not patriotism, sold clothes.

Press Week changed the way Americans considered and consumed fashion. Although 80 percent of the dresses sold in the United States were made in New York City, most American women—and fashion journalists—looked to Paris for guidance. Manufacturers, too, were complicit in this exchange, paying fees, or "cautions," to French couture houses for the right to copy their designs. Press Week served as a timely reminder that New York had its own ideas to offer—more than ever, now that it was not able to copy or expected to compete with Paris. Lambert brought America's fashion reporters to New York en masse, to be dazzled by the collective creativity and skill of Seventh Avenue. To ensure their enthusiastic participation, Lambert arranged for journalists' travel expenses to be paid and ensured that a good time was had by all—orchestrating, for example, cocktail parties with the New York fashion press, audiences with Mayor Fiorello LaGuardia, and tickets to Broadway shows.

Lambert "was the first one—the only one—to organize Seventh Avenue," according to one fashion editor. "No one had ever done it before. No one had even *thought* of doing it."[24] Previously, regional reporters had shadowed hometown buyers—the influential gatekeepers who decided what got sold in department stores and specialty boutiques nationwide—as they placed orders in Seventh Avenue showrooms. Instead of informal viewings, Lambert staged fashion shows—or "mannequin parades," as they were called then—like those regularly held by French couture houses for clients and journalists, subtly elevating American ready-to-wear to the status of Parisian couture. By 1957, *Vogue* was using the term *American chic* to describe "an easy elegance that rests on well-groomed, simple lines." American women, it acknowledged, were developing "a sixth sense of chic" characterized by "ease of putting together clothes that are essentially uncomplicated in themselves."[25] By applying a French word—*chic*—to homegrown American style, the magazine implicitly acknowledged that New York was now a serious rival to Paris.[26]

Press Week was just one of Lambert's many innovations. In 1940, she revived the International Best Dressed List as a New York (rather than Paris) institution. In 1941, she partnered with the cosmetics firm Coty to establish the Coty Awards, fashion's equivalent of the Oscars. In 1947, she organized the first Party of the Year, the annual Costume Institute fundraiser now known as the Met Gala. In 1962, she founded the Council of Fashion Designers of America. In 1964, she began writing a syndicated weekly fashion column, which ran for 40 years. And, in 1965, President Johnson appointed her to the first National Council on the Arts, the advisory group for the newly established National Endowment for the Arts. It was the fulfillment of her dream of making fashion recognized as an art form on the national stage. As Oleg Cassini reflected, "it was as if she had opened a school to teach fashion to the rest of the country."[27]

If anyone could teach fashion to Mrs. Johnson, it was Eleanor Lambert. On February 15, 1966, she wrote to the First Lady with a proposal:

> I am sending this note in the very sincere hope that sometime in March or April you might be willing to give me a brief appointment to discuss the prospect of—someday, at a more quiet moment in history—having a presentation of the American Art of fashion in The White House or at the Corcoran Gallery under your direct patronage.
>
> American fashion is long overdue to assume a place of honor among creative forces of our culture. As you know, the situation is reversed in most other countries, even Russia. Through this fact Great Britain, Spain, Italy, Ireland, France, Thailand and others are steadily building up their export revenue by putting an official aura around their couture.
>
> As you see, I'm on my soapbox. But if you are at all interested in discussing it with me, I shall be tremendously grateful for even a few moments.

Instead of writing directly to the First Lady, however, she sent the letter to Bess along with a pair of Nina Ricci stockings and a note:

> I enclose, for your decision, a note to Mrs. Johnson asking flat out for the opportunity to present my reasons for hoping for a White House fashion show next winter, or at least after these tense days are past. She is always so interested in whomever she meets that perhaps I am presumptuous in thinking she would be willing to hear me out personally for a few minutes. But anyway, I'd like to try. If you don't agree, you know best. . . . P.S. And don't tell me I'm trying to bribe you with nylons![28]

There is no evidence that Abell gave the letter to Mrs. Johnson. The Vietnam War was at a critical phase: six weeks of peace negotiations broken by the biggest US offensive to date, Operation Masher. Even if Mrs. Johnson had received the letter, it would not have been surprising if she failed to act on it, with so many other concerns pressing on her. "As a member of the National Council of the Arts, Eleanor Lambert did her best to talk a show of American fashions into the White House," syndicated fashion columnist Eugenia Sheppard would later claim. "In spite of the booming industry behind the lightminded business of clothes, the conservatives held out. A fashion show was for some other place."[29] But Lambert was not easily dissuaded, and neither was Abell.

Six months later, in August 1966, Dickerson sent Abell a newspaper article about Lambert's pet project, the Council of Fashion Designers of America. In her accompanying letter, Dickerson referred to the group as "the one we talked about when we discussed a possible fashion show at the White House. I still think that's a great idea—and that you ought to reinstigate it. From her personal and public viewpoints, I think this would be great for Mrs. Johnson." She added: "And wouldn't it drive *Women's Wear Daily* nuts?"[30] The First Lady had just banned the publication from covering Luci's August 6 wedding after its reporters broke into Priscilla of Boston's premises and published a sketch of the wedding gown, leaving Luci "woefully distressed." ("Personally, I didn't think it was any great matter," said Mrs. Johnson.)[31]

Just over a month later—right after Mrs. Johnson returned from her West Coast trip—Dickerson wrote to her directly, gushing about a benefit ballet-fashion show she had seen in New York. Lambert had produced the event, which featured clothes from 30 American collections selected by Norman Norell; Mrs. Kennedy had served as honorary chair.[32] "Since it is a general consensus that American designers have now caught up with and perhaps this year overtaken the Parisian haute couture, why wouldn't it be a good idea to give American designers some sort of recognition with a White House setting?" she asked. "As you know, the American fashion business is our fifth largest industry." She proposed it as "a possible idea for showing a visiting dignitary or perhaps all of the ambassadors' wives. . . . I know all the fashion people in New York could come up with something equally original and snappy for presentation here."[33] Bess appended her own note to the letter: "I would still like to do something like this for the wives of Ambassadors. Do you still feel its something you want to keep hands off?" Apparently it was: once again, the idea languished for another year and a half.

Decades later, Bess Abell took credit for finally making the event happen. "I didn't immediately win over Mrs. Johnson right away, because she thought of fashion as too froufrou," she said. "It wasn't! It made a difference when I pointed out that fashion was a big business for the U. S. of A., and at the point she was on board.”[34] By 1968, fashion had grown to be the fourth largest industry in the United States, employing 1.4 million Americans, more than 80 percent of them women.[35] Indeed, the garment industry was the country's largest employer of women.

Less than a month before assuming the presidency, LBJ had taken a well-publicized walking tour of the congested Seventh Avenue garment district with International Ladies' Garment Workers' Union president David Dubinsky, visiting Abe Schrader's factory and Norman Norell's showroom. "He shook a lot of hands, smiled at a lot of people and made the day unforgettable for workers who never imagined that a vice-president of the United States would someday visit them where they work. . . . A babble of Yiddish, Spanish, Italian, and English filled the air with remarks of admiration for both men." LBJ called it "one of the most enjoyable days I've ever spent."[36] His visit was the talk of the industry for weeks afterward.

It was an industry that was becoming politically active. On December 6, 1967, a working group of designers and manufacturers, including Jerry Silverman, Malcolm Starr, Pauline Trigère, and Chester Weinberg, called a meeting of the major Seventh Avenue players—most of them represented in the fashion show—to discuss a boycott of French couture and French textiles, in response to General De Gaulle's recent anti-American and anti-Israeli statements. "De Gaulle's timing could not have been worse for the French fashion industry," *Women's Wear Daily* reported. "Even before he stirred up animosity, buying at the couture houses has been falling off and the line-for-line copies didn't sell well last season." Though the boycott never materialized, the United States could credibly threaten the French without risking its own bottom line, thanks to improvements in Swiss and Italian textile manufacturing—and the rise of homegrown firms like Chardon-Marché.[37] Seventh Avenue was tired of playing second fiddle to Europe. The time was right to celebrate American designers.

The midwinter meeting of the National Governors' Conference was scheduled for February 1968. "We needed a time that Mrs. Johnson would be happy with to have the show so it seemed perfect to do for the governor's wives and call it 'Discover America,'" Abell remembered.[38] In early February, the First Lady issued invitations and handwritten White House security passes for a luncheon presentation of spring fashions to entertain the governors' wives, titled "How to Discover America in Style." The date was set for February 29, 1968 (it was a leap year). Originally, the vast East Room was considered as a possible venue, but it would be needed for the post-dinner entertainment that night; the smaller but more symbolic State Dining Room was chosen instead.[39]

The show was conceived as a joint boost to America's garment industry and President Johnson's pet project, domestic tourism. Launched in April

1967 by presidential proclamation, the Discover America program aimed to raise awareness of "the benefits which travel in the United States will bring to the Nation, its citizens and its visitors"—not least among them an estimated $26 billion per year benefit to the American economy.[40] The advent of commercial jet travel had made foreign travel an affordable option for Americans. The Boeing 707 made its maiden voyage in 1958, offering commercial service between the United States and Europe. That year, for the first time, more people crossed the Atlantic by air than by sea. In 1967, 3.3 million Americans vacationed abroad, while only 1.5 million foreigners visited the United States.[41] The President aimed to stem the so-called dollar drain by encouraging Americans to spend their vacation budgets on domestic travel. "The fashion show has become an instrument of economic policy," the *Washington Post* observed.[42]

Designer Rudi Gernreich's fashion show invitation and handwritten security pass (Courtesy of the FIDM Museum at the Fashion Institute of Design & Merchandising, Los Angeles, CA, Rudi Gernreich Archive, Bequest of the Rudi Gernreich Estate)

"Discover America" dovetailed nicely with Mrs. Johnson's own platform, highway beautification, a cause she had taken up on the many long, litter-strewn drives from Texas to Washington the Johnsons made during LBJ's congressional terms. As First Lady, she extended "beautification" beyond America's highways to city planning, parks, gardens, and conservation. "To me, it was always just part of the whole broad tapestry of environment—clean air, clean water, free rivers, the preservation of scenic areas."[43] Later in life, after she had left the White House, she would be recognized as "one of the first crusaders for ecology"; today, she would be called an environmentalist.[44] As Sharon Francis, Mrs. Johnson's assistant for beautification and conservation, remembers, "she was always slightly uncomfortable with the word 'beautification,' as it could be interpreted as being more trivial than her aim of incorporating natural beauty into the cities and neighborhoods of everyday life, as well as preserving deserving wild places in the hinterlands."[45] While fashion and the National Parks Service may seem like strange bedfellows, both Seventh Avenue and the tourist industry benefited from the postwar impetus to celebrate America as not just equal to but better than Europe—a task given renewed urgency by the unpopular Vietnam War.

The First Lady with her staff—Liz Carpenter, Bess Abell, and Ashton Gonella—on January 17, 1969, in the last days of the Johnson administration (LBJ Library photo by Yoichi Okamoto)

Though the idea of a fashion show at the White House had by now been in the air for almost three years, it came together in a mere three weeks. Such a feat of logistics would be impressive today. That it happened in the era of telegrams and mimeographs is nothing short of astonishing—a testimony to both the fast pace of life at 1600 Pennsylvania Avenue and the power of the Executive Office. Sheaves of memos, guests lists, security clearances, and seating charts carefully archived in the five floors of air-conditioned stacks at the Lyndon Baines Johnson Presidential Library illuminate the complexity of the event as well as the collective anxiety over getting it right. It was, the *Chicago Tribune* reported, "an event more complicated than a military maneuver"—a bold claim in wartime.[46]

Ultimately, the fashion show was the brainchild of several prominent and powerful women, all with competing agendas: Dickerson, the famous newscaster; Lambert, the well-connected fashion publicist; and Abell, the First Lady's social secretary. Liz Carpenter and her staff acted as media liaisons for the many invited journalists. In addition, Lambert formed an advisory committee chaired by *Harper's Bazaar* editor Nancy White and consisting of a "bipartisan" team of three Washington-based fashion editors: Eleni Epstein of the *Washington Star*, Dorothy LeSueur of the *Washington Post*, and Nina Hyde of the *Washington Daily News*.[47]

Harper's Bazaar and its archrival, *Vogue*, were the two premier American fashion magazines of the 1960s. Nancy White had inherited the editor-in-chief job from her aunt, the legendary Carmel Snow, in 1958—an appointment that caused White's colleague Diana Vreeland to quit and flee to *Vogue*.

Unlike Vreeland, White "did not operate by personality and do eccentric things," Lambert said of her. She was a traditionalist—always impeccably groomed, with her white gloves and hat in place. But she was known for giving *Harper's Bazaar* a modern, artsy look, recruiting top photographers while fostering young design talent. Shepherding the magazine through a period of tremendous social and sartorial change, she once staged a fashion shoot at Cape Canaveral, and she commissioned artsy photographs of birth control pills.[48] White already had a relationship with the White House; she had recently replaced Lambert on the National Council on the Arts. She was also a childhood friend of Katharine Graham, the president of the *Washington Post*.[49] (Vreeland was invited to the White House fashion show, but she did not attend; *Vogue* made no mention of the event.)

Epstein, born Helen Sakes, was just 21 when she was named fashion editor of the *Star*. But she considered herself a serious journalist. "I cover fashions just like another reporter would cover the White House," she once said. At 5'2", not including her towering mane of black hair, she favored tailored black suits—particularly Pauline Trigère's—and jewelry inspired by her Greek heritage.[50] A DC native, she was defensive about the city's frumpy reputation. "I'm tired of that cliché about Washington women being dowdy," she once said. "The transplants who come here with each new administration might start that way, but they quickly shape up once their figures and faces start appearing in the newspapers."[51]

Dallas-born Dorothy LeSueur was fairly new to the *Post*, having been hired away from the *New York Times* in October 1966. Her husband, Larry LeSueur, had won the Medal of Freedom for his war reporting for CBS, and he was the White House correspondent for the Voice of America radio service.[52] LeSueur would leave the paper in 1972, amid complaints that "fashion is a dirty word at the *Post*."[53]

Native New Yorker Nina Hyde would take Le-Sueur's job at the *Post* after the *Daily News* went out of business. She was known for weaving political and social commentary into her fashion coverage. Hyde was "the best of the bunch," Abell remembers. "That's awful for me to say, but I thought Nina was the smartest and most serious, and as I remember she was the only one who wouldn't buy on the cheap directly from designers."[54] Hyde, who had worked for *Women's Wear Daily* before coming to Washington, disagreed with Epstein's assessment of Capitol style. "There is an awful lot of safe dressing here," she observed.[55]

Nina Hyde, fashion writer for the *Washington Daily News,* making last-minute alterations to the fashion show lineup; her notes are preserved in the LBJ Library. (LBJ Library photo by Robert Knudsen)

It was the committee's job to select the clothes, accessories, props, and models and to arrange for everything to be delivered from New York to Washington in time for the event. Surviving memos suggest that though LeSueur, Epstein, White, and Hyde had equal influence over the choice of designers and garments, other duties were divvied up; Epstein shepherded the models, while Hyde handled accessories, props, and hotel arrangements.

White and her staff at *Harper's Bazaar* pulled a reported 400 pieces from the spring collections, which the committee vetted in Eleanor Lambert's office the week before the show.[56] "We spent whole days in New York picking, discarding, calling for more, discarding again," one committee member remembered.[57] With only half an hour allotted for the presentation—the standard time limit for any entertainment in the Johnson White House—they planned to winnow the selection down to 50.[58] (Tellingly, a stopwatch was among the supplies the First Lady's office requisitioned for the show.)[59] In the end, 100 outfits made the journey to DC, of which approximately 88 appeared on the runway in rapid succession.[60] "They won't all be high-priced couture levels," Eleni Epstein told the *Chicago Daily News.*[61] White offered a reporter some insights into the selection process. She justified showing some "very young" looks to the mature ladies in the audience: "We felt they might be interested in something for their children."[62] Indeed, the *Philadelphia Inquirer* would later observe that "most of the clothes on the runway looked more suitable for Lynda Robb and her generation than for most of the guests."[63] The governors' wives were a conservative bunch even by Mrs. Johnson's standards; in 1967, she regretted instituting a black-tie dress code for a gubernatorial dinner party because "in general . . . I knew it well the Governors and their wives are likely to be low-key dressers."[64] The committee members—more attuned to New York and the Beltway than the state capitals of America—may have misjudged their audience.

Meanwhile, Abell and Carpenter managed the logistics at the White House, sourcing mirrors, sewing machines, ironing boards, lights, makeup tables, garments racks (eventually borrowed from the Mayflower Hotel), a stopwatch, and everything else needed to mount a New York–style fashion show in the gold and white State Dining Room. George K. Payne, the display director of DC department store Woodward & Lothrop, erected a white-carpeted, 600-foot, U-shaped runway for the occasion.[65] On February 27, a van left the White House garage to pick up a painting that had been sent to New York for restoration and cleaning; at the same time, it collected several boxes and suitcases of clothes, shoes, hats, and accessories from Lambert's office.[66]

A final member of the team was Frankie Welch, who owned an eponymous boutique in the Washington suburb of Alexandria, Virginia, which was frequented by congressional wives and carried clothes by many designers

Frankie Welch at work on the Discover America scarf (LBJ Library photo by Robert Knudsen)

that would be represented in the fashion show.[67] Though Welch would become famous for the scarves and scarf-dresses she designed herself—often commissioned by political campaigns and organizations—at the time, she had only produced one.[68] In 1966, Virginia Rusk—the wife of Dean Rusk, the secretary of state under Presidents Kennedy and Johnson—asked Welch to create an "all-American design" for a scarf Rusk could give to visiting dignitaries. Welch drew on her Native American heritage and the history of Rusk's home state of Georgia and came up with her iconic Cherokee Alphabet.[69] It was likely this scarf that gave Bess Abell and Liz Carpenter the idea to commission Welch to design a red, white, and blue souvenir scarf for the fashion show guests.

In January 1967, Eugenia Sheppard had noted the fad for "signature scarfs": scarves emblazoned with a designer's name, an early incarnation of the visible designer label. "To own a collection—nobody I know can bear to stop at one—is like owning a little collection of art," Sheppard asserted. "It is also like getting to know the designer himself. A scarf is far more of a giveaway to the personality behind any of this country's top fashion labels than the clothes themselves. The clothes have been carefully planned for selling, but the scarfs have been tossed off spontaneously in a relaxed, amused moment."[70] The First Lady was in the habit of giving signature scarves by American designers as diplomatic gifts. "The wives of foreign heads of state who have received signature scarves from Mrs. Johnson have been greatly pleased," Abell testified.[71]

Abell contacted Welch in early February. "She came to my office," Abell recalls. "As I remember, it was late afternoon and she took a taxi back to her

Left: Cherokee Alphabet scarf, by Frankie Welch, 1966 (Author's collection)

Right: Discover America scarf, by Frankie Welch, 1968 (Author's collection)

place on Cameron Street. She called me and said: 'I designed this scarf in the back of the taxi and you're going to love it.' She said: 'The taxi driver really likes it.' Frankie's scarf was the 'Discover America' scarf."[72] The 22-inch square scarf featured an abstract map of the continental United States, with the Great Lakes in blue and the words "Discover America" in red. Welch pointed out that "red, white and blue and one initial show any way you tie it—which I think is fun."[73] Initially, Abell and Carpenter planned to have 50 scarves made, but Abell doubled the order as she "thought Mrs. Johnson would want each member of the press and each designer present at the luncheon to have one."[74] Welch made 20 extra, so they could be worn on the runway as well.

Because she had barely three weeks to create 120 scarves, Welch hand-painted and screen-printed them with the help of a small army of volunteers "from grandfathers to teen-agers," recruited with the help of a television ad; she even pressed the taxi driver, Roy Fahnestock, into service. "Some of the scarves were scarcely dry" on the day of the show, the *Los Angeles Times* reported.[75] Each guest, designer, and member of the press received one, and the extras appeared on the runway in the form of umbrellas, banners, hats, and other accessories.[76] The guests were promised a printed, colorfast version to replace the hand-painted one, but several of the original painted scarves survive today, including one in the Denver Public Library, claimed by the governor of Colorado's wife.[77]

It was always the intention to have the "Discover America" scarves mass-produced for sale; they would be available two weeks after the luncheon. Liz Carpenter had the bright idea of selling them in National Parks gifts shops as well as department stores.[78] Welch, a Georgia native, even produced one customized with a background repeating "See Georgia First" for the state's welcome center hostesses.[79] The White House ordered several to be given as gifts to visiting dignitaries; they were also distributed to the female foreign journalists who accompanied Mrs. Johnson on her April 1968 "Discover America with the First Lady" tour of Texas.[80] But internal

Frankie Welch and her team of volunteers hand-painting, screen-printing, and ironing Discover America scarves for the fashion show guests at Duvall House, Welch's Alexandria home and boutique (LBJ Library photos by Robert Knudsen)

correspondence preserved in the Johnson Presidential Library reveals what was kept a closely held secret at the time: the printed version of the scarf was designed and produced by legendary textile designer Julian Tomchin and his assistant Steve Wysocki, of the textile firm Chardon-Marché. Tomchin's involvement was deliberately kept quiet because he and Wysocki were Republicans.[81] Welch made sure that they were not invited to the fashion show, as it could have proved embarrassing for Mrs. Johnson.

Tomchin's participation, however, was seen as a way to lure Nancy White onto the advisory committee. As Welch pointed out to Abell, White "has been known for so many years for the wonderful ways she ties a scarf and I know she would use the scarf in several clever ways in the show. Also, she will respect the fact that Julian Tomchin's design is being used on the scarf—since he is really our top fabric designer in the United States. *Harper's Bazaar* always gives him credit lines and pictures in the magazine."[82]

Was the elaborate tale of Welch designing the scarf in the back of a taxi actually true? Perhaps she came up with the concept, then handed it over to Tomchin for execution? Did he simply adapt her hand-painted design for mass-production? Or was the design his all along? Later in her scarf-making career, Welch would come up with basic concept and work with an artist to finalize the design; this may have been the case with Tomchin and the "Discover America" scarf.[83] The scarf, highly collectible today, has always borne Frankie Welch's signature, "F. W. of Va." And shortly after the show took place, Welch began selling a second, rectangular version of the scarf made up of eight-inch-square repeats, as well as caftan-like maxi dresses and knee-length skirts using yardage printed with the "Discover America" design. The bipartisan dress was worn by "several candidates' campaigners" during the 1968 election season.[84] Libby Cater, the wife of LBJ aide Douglass Cater, modeled one for the *New York Times*, and another appeared in a 1971 fashion show held at the US consulate general in Willemstad, Curaçao.[85] Welch even sent one of the dresses to Mrs. Johnson, but Abell returned it with a note reading: "The dress is really delightful. . . . Mrs. Johnson thought it quite attractive—and it fit very well—but she felt it was a bit young for her."[86] But she did not begin painting the souvenir scarves until Julian Tomchin had completed the official design and his assistant had sent it to the White House "to use as a blow up, or any way you wish."[87]

The flurry of careful preparations is all the more impressive because there was no budget for the show. Lambert and the committee members volunteered their time. Many of the planners and participants likewise donated their time and services, including Jackie Kennedy's hairdresser Jean-Paul Amsellem of the Jean-Paul et Norbert salon in Georgetown. New York's Mannequin agency, run by ex-model Gillis MacGil, provided 12 $250-a-day models at no charge. Six of the designers represented in the show—Samuel Winston, Mollie Parnis, Bill Blass, Donald Brooks, Oscar de la Renta, and James Galanos—also lent their salaried house models.[88] Sheffield, the watchmaker, underwrote part of the event's costs; in return, guests received a customized Sheffield promotional brochure. On the day of the show, "a reporter shouted a question about who was paying for it, but there wasn't very much to pay for."[89]

A week before the show was to take place, the *Washington Post* hinted that the White House and the committee had conflicting agendas, with the First Lady pushing for affordable clothes that were "wearable, not weird" and the committee focused on promoting elite American designers—most of them Lambert's clients.[90] (This was not necessarily nepotism; as the only specialist fashion publicist in America, Lambert represented virtually the entire industry.) As Sharon Francis remembers, Mrs. Johnson originally envisioned the show as "a way to showcase good-looking, outdoorsy clothes. That, of course, was not where the fashion industry was investing its creative talents."[91] In initial discussions, "it was hoped that the emphasis would be on travel clothes," the *Post* reported. But "designers see the show not as a spur to American travel but as a breakthrough for the American fashion industry."[92] Tensions came to a head in a heated phone conversation between Liz Carpenter and Eleanor Lambert on February 21, in which Carpenter informed Lambert "that *all* the final decisions concerning the Fashion Show are being made here at the White House and that we will make all the announcements concerning the luncheon, etc."[93] Nancy White expressed her frustration to the *Post*. "To show only 50 pieces cannot represent the sum of American fashion," she said. "We will make it the best 50 pieces for a given audience that we can put together. The best of American fashion is a whole different subject."[94] Clearly, she was managing expectations.

Through all the preparations, the First Lady seems to have been largely absent, occupied by her usual packed schedule of duties, punctuated by late-night phone calls from the Situation Room as tensions escalated in Vietnam, civil rights activists picketed the White House, and North Korea captured the USS *Pueblo*. On January 18, singer and actress Eartha Kitt embarrassed the First Lady at a White House luncheon focusing on crime and juvenile delinquency by denouncing the Vietnam War; though the media took Johnson's side, they criticized Kitt's manners more than her politics. When Johnson attended the reopening of the Woman's National Democratic Club a week later, antiwar activists were waiting with signs supporting Kitt. "These hellish days," the First Lady mused on February 6, with an uncharacteristic note of pessimism. "Fractious factions everywhere, Southeast Asia, the Senate, segments of our own country." The first mention of the show in her diary came on February 15, when she attended a dinner dance at her friend Mary Lasker's house in New York in the company of several "friends in the

Protestors surround the First Lady as she leaves the Women's National Democratic Club on January 24, 1968. (CSU Archives/Everett Collection/Bridgeman Images)

designing world, cute Mrs. Richard Raines, Adele [Simpson]'s daughter. Mollie Parnis and her son; and several who are helping us put on the style show, for the governors' wives. Nancy White of *Harper's,* and I think, Eleanor Lambert."[95] The show was not formally announced to the press until February 21.[96]

Apart from vague references to "working hard," the diary is silent on the subject of the show until February 28. "This was a day that ran the full gamut of emotion, from tears to laughter," the First Lady reflected. "A day of grinding work and robot hand shaking, and people and events crowding every hour." Most of these people and events were unrelated to the fashion show; there were several houseguests to welcome—including Lynda and her husband—and the everyday business of the White House continued even as models, editors, and hairdressers arrived from New York. The president's schedule included meetings with his cabinet, with the Human Rights Commission, the Inter-American Council of Commerce and Production, the governors, the president's dermatologist, and more—all in the White House.[97]

At 8:00 A.M., two men from the White House garage unloaded the New York van at the Northwest Gate Service Entrance. The 5'x3'x2' packing crates of clothes had to be carried up two floors to the Queen's Bedroom and Lincoln Bedroom.[98] "The White House had not realized how much space would be needed for all the clothes and the accessories for each costume, the wiglets, the shoes, hats, jewelry, and gloves," a member of the committee revealed.[99] On the first floor, the U-shaped runway was being erected in the State Dining Room.

In the midst of all this, the First Lady spent her morning trying on dresses to choose the one in which she would welcome dozens of America's

Models (*from left*) Toni Bailey, Helen Hite, and Harriet Simmell joined Mrs. Johnson for a photo call on the South Lawn on the day before the fashion show. (Courtesy of Frankie Welch, Peggy Welch Williams, and Genie Welch Leisure)

Toni Bailey and Mrs. Johnson at the photo call (LBJ Library, White House Naval Photographic Unit, Outs Roll 15 of 16 of MP 893, *The President, February 1968*)

top fashion designers to the White House. "Tomorrow the Governors and their ladies will be here for the style show I'm having for the ladies," she recorded in her diary. "I will need a white dress that will show off the red, white and blue scarf with the 'Discover America' motif, so I tried on a number, chose one, worked with Liz."[100] She selected a knee-length white wool shirt-dress with gold buttons whose designer she diplomatically refused to name, explaining: "I wanted the day to be representative of all designers."[101] ("I wouldn't dare say who designed it," Carpenter told reporters, laughing.)[102] The question of the dress settled, the First Lady and Carpenter had a hurried lunch of scrambled eggs on trays in her room, then rushed downstairs for an emotional ceremony in which the president presented the Medal of Freedom to Robert McNamara, who, as the country's longest-serving secretary of defense, had guided America through the Cuban Missile Crisis and into the Vietnam War.[103] McNamara was leaving the cabinet to become president of the World Bank; though he went willingly, the timing of his departure—in advance of Johnson's expected bid for reelection—suggested that his departure was motivated by political expediency. The secretary, who had faced harsh criticism as well as plaudits during his seven-year tenure, testified: "[The President] was very, very warm in his comments" in the "very beautiful ceremony at the White House. . . . I became so emotional, I could not respond."[104]

Mrs. Johnson, too, was overcome with emotion. After saying good-bye to the McNamaras, she went back upstairs to the family quarters and promptly broke down in tears. "But it was a short few moments because I had to get into a dress, to be photographed with the models for the 'Discover America' style show tomorrow, down on the South Lawn."[105] In the awkward photo op, the 5'4" First Lady in her knee-skimming ivory dress could not help looking short and matronly next to the three tall, miniskirted models clad in brilliant red, white, and blue. But she put on a brave face as she posed and chatted for the cameras. No one would ever guess that moments earlier she had been crying her eyes out.

3

The Models

The three models who joined Mrs. Johnson on the South Lawn that morning were not the $250-per-day Mannequin models from New York. They were local models recruited from the Washington, DC, area by Nina Hyde: Toni Bailey (in a Discover America hat), Helen Hite (who twirled an umbrella made of the Discover America scarf fabric), and Harriet Simmell (in a Discover America headscarf). Alexandria-based Simmell had modeled Frankie Welch's Cherokee Alphabet dress at the Northern Virginia Art Museum the previous year and may have been recommended by the designer.[1] Bailey, of Baltimore, was born Maria Antoinette Musiani in Naples, Italy. Hite was famed for her "wicked sense of humor" and her resemblance to Mrs. Johnson's daughter Lynda; she was often mistaken for the First Daughter as she shuttled between her home in the capital and New York, where she modeled for B. H. Wragge, Donald Brooks, Sarmi, and Oscar de la Renta. "I don't look like her," the 5'9" brunette joked. "She looks like me!" The two shared a Norwegian hairdresser—Eivind of Saks Fifth Avenue—and Texas roots.[2] A 1967 interview with "Lynda Bird's double" revealed that "she keeps her figure by shunning food."[3] Additional local girls were recruited to help out as models and behind the scenes. Ponytailed Bonnie Pfeifer, a Maryland Catholic high school student, she had been part of DC department store Hecht Company's "teen board" when she was "discovered" by Dorothy LeSueur in a local charity fashion show; her mother let her cut class to model at the White House.[4] She was so inexperienced that the organizers gave her "walking lessons" and did her makeup for her, while the professional models did their own. The Mannequin models "didn't even talk to me—I was just this local kid," she remembers. "I was terrified!"[5]

Models (*from left*) Toni Bailey, Helen Hite, and Harriet Simmell with the First Lady at a photo call on the South Lawn on the day before the fashion show (NARA)

Madeleine Little was another long-haired blonde and LeSueur protégé; by 1969, she was working for her as a model and editorial fashion assistant at the *Washington Post*. Alexandra Creel Tufo, the scion of a powerful New York family and wife of a Washington lobbyist, had a similar arrangement, modeling for the paper's fashion pages while also writing articles; however, while she was issued a security pass, she does not appear to have modeled in the show and may have been there as a dresser. Dianne Waters, from Virginia, was a student at Georgetown University; Frances Conden studied at Mount Vernon Junior College.

Most of the remaining models—the Mannequin girls and the New York–based house models—flew down from New York on an American Airlines shuttle that afternoon (some of them remember arriving early the next morning). At 4:00 P.M., a chartered bus dropped them off at the White House for what would prove an intense round of fittings.[6] (By that time, Mrs. Johnson had received a delegation from the Business and Professional Women's Foundation in the Library and moved on to the Blue Room, where she hosted a tea for 300 members of the National Council of Jewish Women.)[7]

Most of the models were in their teens or twenties at the time and were at the forefront of the counterculture that was about to shake the nation. Some had boyfriends stationed in Vietnam; others were adamantly antiwar (and, consequently, anti-LBJ). Some were moonlighting students; others were established professionals. (In many cases, the pros could be recognized by their cropped hairstyles, which were easy to alter with hairpieces—even mid-show.)[8] Today, some have fond memories and cherished photos and souvenirs of their visit to the White House. Others have no memories of it at all; glamorous locations came with the job, and any distinct impressions have been eroded by time and the aging process.

MacGil had begun her career as a stock girl in the Bergdorf Goodman lingerie department. She started doing fashion shows in the store, then embarked on a two-decade international modeling career. "She looked so much like Jackie [Kennedy] that she was in constant demand for New York shows," Barbara Cloud, the fashion editor of the *Pittsburgh Press*, noted.[9] That may be why MacGil was selected to wear a Jackie-style boxy blue suit, red pillbox hat, and white gloves on a politically themed *Vogue* cover of 1962. "She was a supermodel long before that term existed," according to her *Women's Wear Daily* obituary.[10] Her relationship with Lambert—and luminaries such as Blass, Beene, Norell, Trigère, Galanos, and Arnold Scaasi—dated back to her own modeling days. In 1960, she created Mannequin, Inc., the first agency specifically for "show" or runway models, operating out of rented office space inside Henri Bendel's Fifth Avenue flagship.[11] "These girls are not the models seen in fashion magazines," the *Wilmington News Journal* explained. "They do little or no photography, which is a specialized work of its own. They are generally a little prettier, avoiding the lean angular look and jutting slouch so favored by high fashion

Left: Models (*from left*) Toni Bailey, Harriet Simmell, and Helen Hite with the First Lady at a photo call on the South Lawn on the day before the fashion show (NARA)

Right: Model Toni Bailey wearing an Emme hat customized with Frankie Welch's Discover America scarf (NARA)

Gillis MacGil channels Jackie Kennedy, surrounded by the rubberized faces of world leaders on the cover of the March 1962 "International Issue" of *Vogue*. (Art Kane/Condé Nast/ Shutterstock)

photographers."[12] Runways meant Press Week but also charity fashion shows, designer showrooms, hotel fashion shows, and special events—such as the White House fashion show—for which the models were paid the same rates as for print work. The typical Mannequin model of the 1960s was between 5'7" and 5'8", with measurements of 34½-25-35; the average print model was slightly taller and slimmer.[13]

The Mannequin models were, and remained, a tight-knit bunch. MacGil kept her roster small by design, beginning with 12 and growing to 60 by 1971.[14] "Because the girls all know each other so well from working together, they are a like a little club," the *News Journal* observed. In contrast to print model agencies, who were always looking for fresh faces, there was little turnover at Mannequin; designers appreciated this consistency from season to season. Also, Mannequin's "girls" tended to be older than print models, "in their late twenties and early thirties."[15] MacGil revealed: "Most of the girls are married, or have been. Most of us are over 25, mature, and simply don't have the time" to go to restaurants or nightclubs.[16] According to Mozella Roberts, MacGil and many of her models were united by their Jewish heritage, though they had adopted Irish or Italian names—a common practice among fashion designers at the time as well.[17] Donald Brooks was born a Blumberg; Norman Norell was originally Norman Levinson; and Arnold Isaacs reversed the letters of his last name to become Arnold Scaasi.

MacGil, then 32, trained her protégées while continuing to work the runway herself.[18] At the time, *mannequin* was the preferred term for what we now call a *model*; like department store dummies, mannequins were expected to be aloof and expressionless, graceful but not animated. That all changed by the end of the 1960s, and *model* replaced *mannequin* in the fashion lexicon. "When I began my career, the ladylike models looked like they belonged to the clothes but stayed discreetly behind them, as if not to upstage them," MacGil remembered. "Then suddenly fashion presentations became show-biz entertainment, with wide runways, raucous rock music, and theatrical lighting effects. And the models themselves became high-stepping, dancing, prancing, strutting, gyrating performers."[19] Instead of fitting a uniform standard of beauty, "none wants to be a carbon copy of any other."[20]

The Mannequin girls were runway models almost exclusively; they rarely appeared in fashion magazines or ads, though some did fittings with designers on a freelance basis.[21] "The fittings, which are the more tiring because the girl has to stand still, are the backbone of a model's income," the *New York Times* revealed—though they paid only half as much per hour as runway modeling. "With a few regular clients, a girl can count on working most of the year, not just at show time." Furthermore, "through her opinions and reactions, she actually influences the course of fashion, which is satisfying."[22] Many of the garments shown on the White House runway were designer samples, made to the measurements of fit models.

The concept of the model as fashion influencer arose out of this close collaboration between models and designers. Mannequin models "look as chic offstage as they do on," one journalist noted.[23] Legendary street style photographer Bill Cunningham wrote in 1968: "If you really want to see what's new, you must keep your eye glued on those curvaceous models, who have the courage to wear with great flair that which the rest of the world dreams about. These are the real trend setters."[24] While the professional models of the previous decade had appeared worldly and womanly, the playful, youthful fashions of the late 1960s demanded fresh faces and lean figures. "Somehow those mini skirts, poor boy sweaters, and Mary Quant dresses just didn't look right on the high-fashion mannequins with their lean bodies and long necks supporting such very aloof faces," New Jersey's *Morning Call* opined. "They looked like socialites clothed in sack cloth.[25] The new breed of model was young—and looked it—but she was no ingenue. Part of her appeal to designers and their customers alike was her innate coolness.

In the tight-knit Seventh Avenue community, the Mannequin models and the house models many designers loaned to the While House fashion show worked together frequently, and their names and faces were familiar to the fashion journalists in the crowd. Many of the models remain friends to this day. Some of the house models had previously worked for Mannequin and other agencies, and some of the Mannequin models (like Judy Dennis, a former house model for Trigère) had worked for individual designers in the show. And house models typically did runway work for other designers during Press Week, alongside agented models. A designer's house model "stands for exactly the way he thinks women ought to look," Eugenia Sheppard revealed. Being a house model was a full-time job—until it wasn't. "Sometimes a designer keeps his key model from one season to other, but it happens more often that the model who was perfection last time begins to look dated the next."[26] Many house models ended up working for agencies after their employers replaced them with new faces and new body types. The Mannequin models chosen to go to White House were selected because they "had a history with the designers" who were showing their clothes there. Though there is no evidence that the designers had a say in which outfits appeared on the runway, the committee made an effort to ensure that they appeared to the best advantage, on preapproved models.[27]

James Galanos liked his models "built like a snake"—long and lean, so thin as to be almost boneless. Once he found a model with that unique body type, he remained loyal to her, using the same lineup of regulars from season to season for his New York showings.[28] Pud Gadiot, one of the models he sent to the White House, had been born in France. In 1952, she met author (and later screenwriter of *Dr. Strangelove, Easy Rider,* and *Barbarella*) Terry Southern, who was studying at the Sorbonne on the GI Bill. They married and moved to the beatnik haven of Greenwich Village in 1953. Though the marriage didn't last, Gadiot found work with Irving Penn and Richard Avedon before being discovered by Galanos. Gadiot was equally loyal to the designer, wearing his clothes on and off the runway. "I get a new outfit whenever I can afford one," she told *New York Times* fashion editor Bernadine Morris in 1966. "Almost everything I have now is by him."[29] The other Galanos model in the show, Chicago native Judy Lawrence, had such a flawless physique that she had served as the model for B. Altman's store mannequins in 1967.[30] In addition to slim, seemingly boneless figures, both models had the "haughty" and "unattainable" look that Galanos felt suited his "elegant and sophisticated" clothes. "I look for a model that looks as though she could be a rich woman," the designer told *New York Times* fashion writer Marylin Bender.[31]

Peggy Parke, the leggy 21-year-old house model for Mollie Parnis—and, before that, Adele Simpson—had already met the First Lady and Bess Abell on several occasions during their shopping excursions to the Carlyle.[32] (She remembers changing behind the clothing rack, knowing that the Secret Service was keeping watch from another building.) "Bess Abell asked me if I was excited about modeling at the White House and I said yes, but it would be strange to do a show without any friends in the audience," she remembered. "She said: 'We're your friends!'"[33] Lynda Hatch—a brunette with a pageboy hairstyle—had also met Mrs. Johnson at the Carlyle during the year and a half she worked as a house model for Parnis. "She was just the loveliest person," Hatch remembers. "I was just this kid—what did she care? But she took the time to actually talk to me and ask me question about my life."[34]

Sherry Thomas was the house model for Donald Brooks. A self-described "simple little girl from New Jersey," she started modeling during her summer

Sherry Thomas models Nat Kaplan's red, white, and blue pleated gown with culotte skirt in rehearsal. (NARA)

vacations at 16, lying about her age. After Brooks replaced her, she eventually went to Mannequin, where she worked alongside many of the models who had joined her on the White House runway.[35]

The oldest and most established model in the Mannequin crew was Denise Linden, a Jackie Kennedy look-alike famous for her close-cropped "tomboy haircut" and naturally lush eyelashes, at a time when most women relied on false lashes.[36] Bernadine Morris called her "one of the most popular girls in her business." Linden had worked for Mollie Parnis before marrying an Air Force captain and taking six years off to raise a family in Columbus, Ohio. When her husband took a civilian job as an investment banker, "I

Models Denise Linden and Jenny Chillcott pose on the landing of Grand Staircase before the show. (LBJ Library, White House Naval Photographic Unit, Outs Roll 16 of 16 of MP 893, *The President, February 1968*)

thought I'd go back to work to help us through the transition," she told the *New York Times*.[37] She was a mother of three when she returned to modeling, and she continued to walk in Parnis's shows each season, adding up to $50 an hour to the family's coffers. Later, she became the house model for Norman Norell, staying with the designer until his death in 1972.

Jenny Chillcott arrived from the United Kingdom in 1964, just as the "London Look" was taking off stateside. At 5'7½", with a boyish figure, enormous blue eyes, and milky skin, she resembled a brunette version of the fashion phenomenon of 1967, Twiggy.[38] MacGil initially refused to sign her because she looked so young.[39] In 1966, she had married a stockbroker and become Jenny Garrigues, though she still used her typically English maiden name professionally; it was good for business. The trip was her first visit to Washington, DC. "I just couldn't believe it," she remembers. "I hadn't been over in America that long, and there I was in the White House with all my pals. It's much smaller than you think! It's a bit more cozy than Buckingham Palace."[40]

Chillcott wasn't the only Brit on the runway that day. Caryl Wilkie, an Englishwoman born in India, had begun her career as a receptionist for Vidal Sassoon in London. The legendary hairdresser had brought her and another one of his "best girls from the London reception team" to New York when he opened his Madison Avenue salon in 1965, "knowing that Americans love hearing a British accent."[41] It was literally a short step from there to the fashion world: the salon was strategically located next door to Paraphernalia, British entrepreneur Paul Young's ultramodern, London-style boutique, which launched the careers of Betsey Johnson and Deanna Littell, among the youngest and hippest designers in the fashion show.

Pat Mori, 5'8", had been with Mannequin since it was formed in 1960.[42] "Her figure is so perfect," the *Wilmington News Journal* reported, that she

Joy Wong, Mozella Roberts, Jenny Chillcott, Sherry Thomas, and Jan Jolley pose on the landing of the Grand Staircase before the show. (NARA)

"is used by many name designers to fit all their sample clothes."[43] Being a fit model was notoriously tedious work, but Mori didn't mind it. "Some girls hate modeling," she told the *New York Times* in 1971. "They feel it's demeaning. . . . But I really love it. It's not just walking around in clothes. You get involved in the clothes that are made on you. You feel you are contributing something."[44]

The Mannequin contingent included two Black models, still something of a novelty on Seventh Avenue. Marylin Bender credited Pauline Trigère with being the first Seventh Avenue designer to hire a Black model, when she made Beverly Valdes her house model in 1961.[45] But Mannequin model Mozella Roberts had been the first Black woman "to get into runway work and make a success of it," according to *Women's Wear Daily*.[46] Born in Winston-Salem, North Carolina, the great-granddaughter of a former slave, and raised in Pittsburgh, Roberts moved to New York in 1953, married, and had two children. In 1959, she separated from her husband and

Denise Linden, Pat Mori, Renée Hunter, Pud Gadiot, Sherry Thomas, Mozella Roberts, Jan Jolley, Jenny Chillcott, and Joy Wong pose on the North Portico before the show. (NARA)

turned to modeling to pay the bills. "Everybody assumed that she was 17," she once said, though she was in her late twenties.[47] "She was an instant hit and has been at the top of the mannequin heap ever since," Eleanor Lambert wrote of the "bubbly" and "exuberant" Roberts in a 1967 column. A onetime house model for Arnold Scaasi, Roberts had "worked for all the big ones" and "works as much as any top white model."[48] Roberts remembered: "For the first five years I was in all kinds of shows without ever seeing another black model on the runway."[49] Indeed, with her light skin and straight hair, she confessed she was rarely asked to model "Afro-American" styles: "Do I look like the type?"[50] But when MacGil recruited her in 1961 and suggested she would get more work if she said she was Polynesian, Roberts refused. "I want to be what I am," she insisted.[51]

But "nobody ever knew that Mozella was a person of color," says Renée Hunter, the only dark-skinned model in the show, who was of mixed Black and Shinnecock Indian descent. "I knew she was, and she knew she was, but no one else ever did."[52] Along with Roberts, Hunter one of just four women of color represented by Mannequin in 1968. Hunter had attended Queens College before becoming a house model for Jacques Tiffeau, whose dress she modeled on the White House runway.[53] While Roberts was signed by Mannequin in 1961 (and, at 29, was one of the oldest models in the show), Hunter had been with Mannequin for less than a year. But she had already worked with many of the designers in the show, including

Red, White, and Blue on the Runway

Models Joan Pavlis, in Samuel Winston, and Fran Healy, in Oscar de la Renta, do their makeup in the Blue Room. (LBJ Library, White House Naval Photographic Unit, MP 893, *The President, February 1968*)

Kasper, Donald Brooks, Adri, and Oscar de la Renta as well as Tiffeau.[54] "As a person of color and a Native American, I was thrilled to be invited to begin with," she says. "I was very privileged and proud to be there."[55]

Fran Healy was known for working with Oscar de la Renta; a 5'8½" redhead, she was the designer's "dream model" and eventually became his house model.[56] Green-eyed Gloria Kirby, a horse-loving former Miss Detroit, attended Wayne State University, majoring in singing, while working her way up in the modeling industry from auto shows to fashion shows. Another former pageant queen, Judy Hinman, née Schaefer, had been runner-up to Miss Minnesota. ("I was too flat," she recalled, though Eugenia Sheppard described her as having "more belle poitrine than the average Seventh Avenue model.")[57] Hinman was a favorite of Rudi Gernreich and bore a striking resemblance to his muse, Peggy Moffitt. In his 1967 resort swimwear show, she had shocked the audience by walking the runway in "an acid green wool diaper and about 25 triangular shiny black stick-on patches. That's all."[58] For Hinman, who preferred the theatricality of the runway to "impersonal" camera work, it just another day at the office. "You must wear a designer's clothes as though they belong to you," she told the *Daily News*.[59]

Beijing-born Joy Wong, a perfect size 6 (meaning size 0, in modern sizing), began modeling in 1960, at age 20, after studying nursing at Johns Hopkins.[60] Her parents had fled China with her "on the last plane" to Hong Kong during the Communist Revolution, moving to Pittsburgh in 1956. But she considered herself a New Yorker. "I love New York," she told the *Daily News*. "I wouldn't trade it for any other city in the world."[61] Wong's exotic beauty was much in demand in a fashion industry hungry for novelty, but Hunter remembers her as being "really perky with a huge smile."[62]

One of the models was actual royalty: Yolande "Yo-Yo" d'Oultremont, the granddaughter of a Belgian count, Paul Cornet du Ways Ruart, and an

Judy Hinman poses for a fall fashion spread in the *Daily News* (New York) wearing a wool coat, gloves, and thigh-high boots on a sweltering day in July 1968. (Jack Smith/*New York Daily News*)

American heiress, Gladys McMillan.[63] Countess d'Oultremont, 28, had modeled for Valentino in Rome and became a house model for Bill Blass after arriving in the United States in 1967.[64] Blass "was into Southampton blondes," remembers Hunter (who never worked for him).[65] At 5'9" and 120 pounds, Yolande bore "a striking resemblance to Candace Bergen."[66]

All the models had to undergo background checks and bag searches before being admitted to the White House. "We weren't expecting such thorough security!" Parke recalled.[67] The models had been instructed to bring their own robes, slippers, and hairpieces. ("Three or four hair pieces are a minimum requirement" for a professional model, the *Morning Call* reported in 1966, "and they must not be inexpensive ones.")[68] Hunter typically traveled with pantyhose and a bodysuit, as girdles were no longer necessary equipment.[69] Chillcott confessed to buying new lingerie every two or three months: "You should be as neat underneath as you are outside; more so when you are stripping all day."[70] As Thomas remembered: "The Secret Service had their hands full searching our bags, between hairpieces and lingerie. I think after a while they just started to reach in without looking."[71] Parke laughed: "Somebody had something in their bag that made the Secret Servicemen blush."[72]

After clearing security, the models were whisked upstairs to the "sacrosanct" Lincoln Bedroom and the Queen's Bedroom, which the White House ushers had outfitted with ironing boards, standing lights, and extra

full-length mirrors.[73] For the rest of the day and well into the early morning, a bevy of beautiful fashion models dashed around the second floor of the White House in their robes while downstairs the busy schedule of meetings, receptions, and ceremonies continued as usual. Indeed, it was even busier than usual, for the White House staff was preparing for not one but three major events the following day: the fashion show luncheon, a black-tie dinner, and a post-dinner performance for the governors and their wives.[74]

Guiding the models through their fittings were the committee members and three of Nancy White's colleagues from *Harper's:* editors Eve Orton, Natalie Gittelson, and China Machado (pronounced CHEE-na). Many of the New York models were already acquainted with the *Harper's Bazaar* team. "They would come to the showrooms in New York all the time," Parke remembers.[75] Nevertheless, they were starstruck by Machado, a stunning former model who was a favorite of Christian Dior's before becoming a fashion editor. "She was so cool," Thomas remembered. "We didn't talk to the editors much, but she was so beautiful. But she was so little! I was always surprised that she modelled on the runway because she was so little."[76] Machado, who was half Chinese and half Portuguese, remembered that she spent the day running around the White House in her standard fashion

Left: Model Harriet Simmell tries on a white Bill Blass coatdress trimmed with black lace from an overstuffed rack in the Lincoln Bedroom; the dress did not appear on the runway. (LBJ Library photo by Robert Knudsen)

Right: A tagged Galanos gown seen on a rack in the Lincoln Bedroom would be one of the final looks in the show. (LBJ Library photo by Robert Knudsen)

A table piled with Kenneth Jay Lane jewelry in the Lincoln Bedroom; sunglasses, scarves, belts, and gloves cover the marble-topped rosewood dresser. (LBJ Library photo by Robert Knudsen)

industry working uniform of head-to-toe black, hoping the Secret Service wouldn't mistake her for the Viet Cong. "Here I am running around all in black," she laughed. "I think they thought I was some Vietnamese woman who had somehow escaped into the White House!"[77]

Five employees of local department stores—Eve Thompson, Elizabeth Said, Mary Pelicano, Chany Jones, and Donna Hecksher—were brought in to help with dressing, pressing, and alterations. At 5:00 P.M., Jean-Paul

Amsellem and his team of hairdressers—Robert Phillips, Robert Gamblin, Lucien Sirqui, and Jacques Duprat—arrived.[78] Liz Carpenter, Bess Abell, and their aides hovered at the ready. In other words, there were as many helpers as there were models crammed into the two second-floor bedrooms, if not more.

The White House was accustomed to hosting heads of state, captains of industry, and stars of the stage and screen. But it had never reckoned with fashion models. One much-discussed topic in the run-up to the show was "What do models eat?" Some of the possibilities suggested included soup, celery, sandwiches, tea, and soft drinks. In this instance, at least, the planners fell short. The *Chicago Tribune* later quoted a committee member saying:

> The White House suddenly realized they were going to have to feed these girls, these 20-something models who had volunteered two days of their time to come down from New York. Bess Abell, the White House social secretary, called me frantically on the phone to ask "What in the world do models eat? Watercress sandwiches?" I told her they eat like vultures, they zero in on food, they live on candy bars and Cokes and everything they can get their teeth into. Even with this warning, the White House couldn't keep up with the girls' appetites. The butlers served tray after tray of ham, cheese, and turkey sandwiches and kept running short. Bouillon flowed like water.[79]

Hunter concurs that "models had the biggest appetite of any people I'd ever seen. Whatever you fed us we ate!" But the White House spread was not very appetizing. "I remember getting a lunch that wasn't so terrific," she says. "We had day-old sandwiches. It wasn't very glamorous for us."[80] Thomas remembers, "All we had were these dried-out sandwiches and consommé. I remember thinking 'This is kind of crappy, to be eating this in the White House.'"[81]

As a member of the advisory committee, Eleni Epstein had privileged access to the behind-the-scenes preparations. "It was bedlam in Lincoln's bedroom as fitting for the first White House fashion show ever presented took place there all day Wednesday," she reported in her story on the show for the *Star*. "Racks, shoes, jewelry, and all the accessories to go with the American fashions were first housed there for fittings prior to being moved down to the Blue Room."[82] Hats blanketed the Great Emancipator's bed. Models swapped outfits while hairdressers, fitters, and editors struggled to create order out of chaos, "stumbling over each other as they attempted to organize each costume with its accessories and proper hair-do to set the whole thing off. (They ended up using big shopping bags to attach all the accessories to the individual dresses)."[83]

In the midst of the confusion, Sherry Thomas spotted a telephone. "I had a friend who lived in Silver Spring, Maryland, and I knew it wouldn't cost anything, so I picked up the phone and started to dial the number," she remembers. "And suddenly I hear 'White House operator, may I help you?' Here I am in all my naiveté. I called my friend and said 'Guess where I'm calling you from? Lincoln's bedroom!'"[84] Peggy Parke joked: "When there was the scandal about people paying to sleep in the Lincoln Bedroom, I thought, 'I got paid money to be in Lincoln's bedroom!'"[85]

Around 11:00 P.M., Captain and Mrs. Charles S. Robb arrived from their home in Arlington; Lynda had moved out of the White House just weeks earlier, after marrying her Marine in the East Room on December 9, 1967. After watching the models for a while, she told her husband: "O.K. Chuck you've seen enough. Anyway we can't afford any new clothes. Let's go."[86]

The president and First Lady returned home from a private party in the early hours of the morning. She had agreed to go out reluctantly, knowing that the following day would be "a sheer tour de force" for both Johnsons. "It was after one o'clock when we reached the White House, and I was surprised to see lights on in the East Room, lights on in the Red and Green Room," Mrs. Johnson recorded in her diary. "Apparently they were

Mrs. Johnson and Mrs. Humphrey posed for a group photo in the moments between the rehearsal and the luncheon; each model received a print inscribed by the First Lady as a souvenir. (Courtesy of Lynda Hatch)

To Lynda Hatch — with deep appreciation and all best wishes
Lady Bird Johnson
February 29, 1968

rehearsing, not for one, but for two entertainments tomorrow. The Style Show and *Fiorello*." The governors and their wives would be entertained by highlights from the Broadway musical *Fiorello* after dinner the following night. Based on the life of New York mayor Fiorello LaGuardia, the 1960 Tony winner was the *Hamilton* of its time: a sweet yet cynical tale of the ups and downs of a political career. "What a marvel Bess is," Mrs. Johnson mused.[87]

The models worked until 2:30 A.M. before departing for their rooms at the Shoreham Hotel, whose restaurant was one of Epstein's regular haunts.[88] But Machado was so tired that she simply collapsed on the bed in the Lincoln Bedroom and slept there among the racks of clothes.[89] The models were due back at the White House at 8:00 A.M. the next morning to prepare for the 9:00 dress rehearsal.

By the time they returned, the White House ushers had moved all the clothes racks to the Blue Room; two 10-foot tables held accessories. The Green Room was converted into a hair salon, with three full-length mirrors and four standing lights.[90] "An SOS went out for mirrors. The White House volunteered their supply of magnifying mirrors which they just happened to have on hand because the President shaves with a magnifying mirror."[91] The ground floor ladies' dressing room—usually used by White House entertainers—was also made available to the models, its usual furniture removed and replaced with empty clothes racks and makeup tables with lighted mirrors.[92] But the show was on the first floor, a quick dash up the grand marble staircase away.

In many ways, the White House fashion show was just another job for the models. The frantic fittings, the last-minute rehearsals, and the suitcases stuffed with makeup, lingerie, and hairpieces went with the territory. But the setting made it extraordinary. "I did a lot of fashion shows over the years, but there's something special about the White House," Parke said.[93]

As the guests were about to arrive, an assistant to Mrs. Johnson came running down from the First Family's living quarters on the third floor and cried: "Who knows how to tie a scarf?" (Scarf-tying virtuoso Nancy White was, apparently, nowhere to be found.) China Machado remembered: "The next minute I'm in [Mrs. Johnson's] apartment and I have to tie her scarf in a way that 'America' shows."[94] That important detail attended to, Mrs. Johnson descended to the State Dining Room, where she watched the final dress rehearsal and posed for a group photo on the runway with the Second Lady, Muriel Humphrey, and the models, still in their finale outfits.[95] Each model would receive a copy signed by Mrs. Johnson: "With deep appreciation and all best wishes." Finally, at 1:00, Mrs. Johnson went to the ground floor to greet her guests.

4

The Guest List

The China Room, where historic White House china was displayed in glass-fronted wall cases lined with red velvet, provided a suitably feminine backdrop for the receiving line. (As Eugenia Sheppard pointed out, space was scarce: between the fashion show and the setup for the black-tie dinner and *Fiorello* performance, "the rest of the White House was hopping.")[1] Standing under the portrait of her predecessor Abigail Adams, the First Lady laughed as she was formally introduced to "Mrs. Robb"—her recently wed eldest daughter.[2]

While her sister, Luci, had always been the family clotheshorse—"No one in the all world liked dresses more than Luci," as Mrs. Johnson put it, with a mix of exasperation and envy—Lynda, too, had "learned to wear clothes with distinction" in the two or three years leading up to the fashion show.[3] Bess Abell attributed Lynda's sudden interest in fashion and makeup to her well-publicized romance with actor George Hamilton, who had received a controversial "hardship exemption" from the draft.[4] In its own waspish way, *Women's Wear Daily* agreed: "George Hamilton may never go to Vietnam. But he has done his bit for his country."[5] Hamilton relished the chance to "play Pygmalion" with Lynda, enlisting Hollywood beautician George Masters to transform her into a "sleek lioness" by deflating her "Dallas bouffant" for a "fresh and natural" hairstyle, arching her eyebrows, and toning down her "oil baroness" makeup. "I sensed that somewhere inside that bookworm was a babe trying to get out," Hamilton wrote in his memoir.[6] But LBJ played his part, too; well before Hamilton came on the scene, Mrs. Johnson observed that Lynda "resents [her father's] determination to make her better groomed, to dress better, and at the same time

Lynda Bird Johnson and George Hamilton leave the El Morocco nightclub in New York on June 23, 1967. (Everett Collection Historical/Alamy Stock Photo)

she rises to the challenge of it."[7] Previously "the unmarried sister with a bookish reputation," Lynda became the family fashion plate.[8]

At 5'10", Lynda wore clothes well. Being younger and less in the public eye than her mother, she could get away with shorter skirts and edgier designers. By 1967, the First Lady testified: "Every time I see her, it's an adventure to see what she has on. She's turning into a regular fashion model." Even Luci looked like a "bargain-basement edition" of her sister at times, their mother confessed. "If I could count the pluses in our lives during the last year, I would place her mastery of the art of dress and grooming, her sense of style, her grace on social occasions, as a very real satisfaction to [her] parents," Mrs. Johnson said of Lynda. "The more so because it is all earned. She didn't begin by having it."[9] Critics sniped that

Lynda's sophisticated new wardrobe was too mature—and expensive—for her tender years; she was only 23 at the time of the fashion show. But they couldn't deny that it was an improvement.

To "Discover America," Lynda chose a chic navy blue Geoffrey Beene coatdress that had been a Christmas present from her father, along with opaque navy stockings; she had worn the same dress to the State of the

Lynda Bird Johnson dressed in Geoffrey Beene for her White House wedding to Marine captain Charles S. Robb on December 9, 1967 (LBJ Library photo by Yoichi Okamoto)

Union address the previous month.[10] (Lady Bird had also received a Beene dress and jacket for Christmas, in yellow wool.)[11] Beene had designed Lynda's medieval-style gown, rehearsal dinner dress, and going-away dress for her December 1967 wedding, as well as her bridesmaids' "Goya red" velvet gowns.[12] The wedding dress, Lady Bird gushed, "fulfilled every expectation. . . . It was, indeed, regal. There was a Renaissance feeling about it, and I hope I live to see a grand-daughter wear it! I am sure it will be just as beautiful then."[13] Lynda's presence at the fashion show instantly upped the cool factor, while significantly lowering the average age of the audience. However, she was—unbeknownst to the many members of the media in the room—in the early stages of her first pregnancy and feeling unwell; today, she has no memory of the event.

In addition to Lynda, the guest list consisted of 35 out of the 54 governors' wives, including representatives from Puerto Rico and the Virgin Islands. (Although there was one female governor in 1968—Alabama's Lurleen Wallace—she was seriously ill with cancer and did not attend the conference.) Most of their RSVPs came on embossed executive mansion stationery, dated February 19 or 20. Thirteen cabinet and administration wives and 26 fashion designers, constituting a who's who of American fashion, also accepted.[14] Including the four committee members, there were 18 journalists scheduled to attend, representing TV, newspapers, magazines, and wire services. Frankie Welch was invited, along with Mrs. Robert Short, whose husband spearheaded the "Discover America" program, and, of course, Eleanor Lambert. In all, 97 people were expected to fill 10 tables for 10, evenly sprinkled with political wives, designers, and journalists. It is probable that Mrs. Johnson also invited Mrs. Kennedy—as well as Mrs. Truman and Mrs. Eisenhower—to the event by phone, before the invitations went out, as was her custom for White House luncheons. But Kennedy never accepted these overtures, finding such events too painful, and on this occasion, neither did Truman or Eisenhower.[15]

While many of the guests followed Mrs. Johnson's lead and wore red, white, and blue in tribute to the "Discover America" theme, they stuck to one or two of the colors rather than wearing all three at once. The First Lady paired her white wool dress from the photo call with navy patent leather shoes and a gold brooch in the shape of a tree flecked with tiny diamonds, a nod to her beautification campaign. Liz Carpenter wore a blue silk cardigan costume by Johnson favorite Adele Simpson, whose work was well represented in the show. Jeanette Rockefeller, wife of the governor of Arkansas, wore a red coatdress with gold buttons; Muriel Humphrey, the vice president's wife, wore a white sleeveless wool dress from Bergdorf Goodman and a white mink hat—one of the few hats in the room. Another one, white and broad-brimmed, could be seen on Betty Williams, wife of the Mississippi governor, paired with a navy blue suit.[16] Miriam Hughes, wife of New Jersey's governor, wore royal blue.[17] Barbara "Toni" Peabody, the "sophisticated, lively," wife of the assistant director of the Office of Emergency Planning, was in white Bill Blass.[18] Frankie Welch wore a red dress with a red, white, and blue scarf. But almost all the guests flew the flag symbolically if not literally, wearing American designers.

Nancy Dickerson, in a yellow and white plaid wool suit by André Courrèges, was "the only woman in the room wearing a French dress,"

Eugenia Sheppard pointed out.[19] She was also one of the few not clad in red, white, or blue. As a major television personality, Dickerson instinctively knew that the way to stand out in a room full of red, white, and blue is to wear yellow. Newsreel footage of the receiving line captured Mrs. Johnson's epic side-eye as she took in Dickerson's out-of-place ensemble. But Dickerson's choice may have sprung from purer motives; although she didn't look it, she was pregnant with her second child. The *Washington Star* would report, "Nancy Dickerson is plan-

Nancy Dickerson wore a yellow André Courrèges ensemble to the fashion show. (LBJ Library, White House Naval Photographic Unit, MP 893, *The President, February 1968*)

ning to go through her present pregnancy mostly wearing Courrèges. His architectural lines are proving just great for her at this time. There will be no maternity fashion as such for her."[20]

Also bucking the red, white, and blue trend was the "tan, fit and curvaceous" Margaretta "Happy" Rockefeller, wife of New York governor Nelson Rockefeller, who had the dubious distinction of being "the most fashionably dressed of the Governors' wives" in a short-sleeved, pale-pink wool jersey dress by Norman Norell, accessorized with an obi sash and a gold and diamond sunburst brooch. (Vera Glaser of the Washington News Service later revealed that Happy had worn pink because she "forgot to pack two dresses" for the Governors' Conference, adding: "Only a Rockefeller could have gotten away with wearing the same dress to the White House she'd had on the night before.")[21] Jane Freeman, wife of the secretary of agriculture, was similarly dressed in peach.[22] And Vera May Williams, the self-described "dowdy" wife of the governor of Arizona, wore a green plaid suit.[23]

There were some notable absences among the Republicans; both Nancy Reagan and Leonore Romney declined the First Lady's invitation. (The night before the fashion show, Romney's husband, Michigan governor George W. Romney, had announced that he was dropping out of the race for the Republican nomination for president, having fallen behind Richard Nixon in the polls.)

Upstairs, the décor of the State Dining Room reinforced the patriotic theme. "Everything was tremendously red, white, and blue," the *Los Angeles Times* observed.[24] The centerpieces, programs, and gilt-edge menus echoed the color scheme. "Each table for eight decorated with red, white and blue criss-crossed ribbons, place cards picturing a girl in an Uncle Sam hat and a wicker basket of red and white sweet peas and carnations, white roses and miniature carnations and blue cornflowers," the *New York Post* reported.[25] The programs were bound with blue cords finished with tassels, to which tiny pencils were attached—just like you'd find at a Press Week fashion show. Only the first two pages were printed, leaving the rest blank for note-taking. "It was just a magnificently done event," Peggy Parke remembers. "The chandeliers, the tables, everything looked so beautiful."[26] Freeman had lunched at White House before but confessed: "I've never been more excited than today."[27]

Initially, Abell hoped to limit the media presence to 15 journalists, but this proved impossible due to the tremendous interest in the event; several reporters who requested credentials were turned down, and others were offered access to the photo call or the rehearsal in lieu of the luncheon. The *Dallas Morning News* was "VERY EXCITED" about the story "for obvious reasons—Neiman Marcus etc."[28] The White House made sure to fill the room with "friendly" reporters; Barbara Coleman of WMAL-TV got invited over Marlene Sanders of ABC, for example, because "she covers us a lot more."[29] All of the journalists were women; with some notable

Joy Wong rehearses in a red, white, and blue outfit by Luba Marks for Elite Juniors in the State Dining Room, where the tables are decorated to match. (Getty Images)

exceptions, like Dickerson and pioneering Cherokee reporter Wauhillau La Hay, who covered the White House for the Scripps-Howard News Service, they were fashion editors or contributors to the "women's page" that was a feature of newspapers at the time. (It "typically covered the four Fs: family, fashion, food, and furnishings.")[30]

Of course, the show had a much larger potential audience: viewers of the monthly Navy Films newsreel *The President*. The fashion show takes up a two-and-a-half-minute snippet in the middle of the February 1968 edition, which can be seen on the LBJ Library's YouTube channel.[31] The sonorous voiceover begins: "A domestic event that took full advantage of the midwinter meeting of the National Governors' Conference was a fashion show and luncheon presented by the First Lady to the governors' wives. Part of a 'Discover America First' campaign, the luncheon's theme focused attention on America's scenic beauty and national heritage." Mrs. Johnson is seen strolling on the South Lawn with three models during the photo call, the South Portico rising in the background. The scene switches to the oval-shaped Blue Room, where models apply makeup in compact mirrors amid racks of clothing as Giuseppe Ceracchi's marble bust of George Washington looks on. "It was the first such fashion show in White House history," the narration continues. "The models prepared themselves in the elegant Blue Room for the performance in the State Dining Room." Shots from the runway and the receiving line follow.

Sportwhirl designer Jeanne Campbell saved her menu, program, invitation, White House security pass, and place card. (Photo by Roy Petersen, Courtesy Jeanie Campbell Petersen)

While the newsreel only depicts a fraction of the show, it is carefully edited for maximum glamour—and patriotism. Virtually all the clothes featured in it are red, white, and blue, though the soundtrack is jaunty lounge music rather than the rousing medley of show tunes and patriotic songs actually provided by the US Marine Band. In reality, glamour and patriotism were at war on the runway, reflecting not just the conflicting agendas of the fashion show's organizers but the fractured state of American fashion—and America itself. The *New York Times* called the event "as patriotic as the Fourth of July, as wholesome as apple pie and as promotional as a TV commercial."[32]

5

The Designers

The White House fashion show united a who's who of designers, from elite "American couturiers" to mass-market manufacturers. Clothes by Seventh Avenue superstars like Bill Blass, Geoffrey Beene, and Donald Brooks—nicknamed the "Three Bs" of American fashion—were presented alongside inexpensive, youth-oriented sportswear brands like Mr. Mort, Ginori, Originala, Sportwhirl, and Junior Sophisticates, the petite clothing label founded by Anne Klein and her husband. Several of the participants had won the Coty Award, fashion's equivalent of the Oscar. The show remains a landmark gathering of American design talent and a rare snapshot of an entire season's worth of Seventh Avenue style. Images and newsreel footage of the show convey the look of 1968 better than any fashion magazine could: an eclectic mix of youth and maturity, couture-quality luxury and mass-market affordability, tradition and innovation. As America teetered on the precipice of a cultural and political revolution, the country's leading creative minds captured the schizophrenic mood.

Unlike the other guests, the designers in the audience received their invitations at the very last minute, only after the committee had made its final selections for the runway. "Even though the telephone calls from the White House social office came in late Tuesday and early Wednesday"—the show was on Thursday—"the designers, rather than being miffed at last minute invitations, are thrilled that American fashion is at last receiving official White House recognition."[1] Sportwhirl designer Jeanne Campbell was so overwhelmed by the invitation that she told a reporter she "couldn't work since receiving it."[2] Though the organizers had planned to select 50 outfits, more than 80 ensembles from nearly 60 different clothing labels were ultimately seen on the runway. Two accessory designers—jeweler Kenneth Jay Lane and shoe designer David Evins—received invitations. Many of the designers "dropped everything to accept the last minute invitation to the historic White House luncheon," reported the *Philadelphia Inquirer*; others, however, had previous engagements or travel plans that they could not escape at such short notice. Deanna Littell, currently living in France, says she didn't get an invitation at all.[3]

Above left: Roxane Kaminstein, seen in a 1963 publicity photo, designed for the Samuel Winston label under her first name. (Author's collection)

Above right: Mrs. Johnson wore this beaded peau de soie Roxane for Samuel Winston gown, purchased at Neiman Marcus, to the 1965 inaugural gala. (Tango Images/ Alamy Stock Photo)

Left: Mrs. Johnson wore the gown several times; she chose it for the State Dinner for President Ayub Khan of Pakistan on December 14, 1965, because "she thought it was Christmasy," a White House spokesman told the *New York Times.* (LBJ Library photo by Robert Knudsen)

The First Lady undoubtedly played a part in the final selection of out-fits, for many of her favorite designers got places of honor on the runway and in the audience. Although she rarely identified the designers of her clothing to the media—and may not always have been cognizant of them herself—eagle-eyed journalists often managed deduce them. "A fashion editor has recognized a Jacques Tiffeau suit and some of his cottons," the *New York Times* reported.[4] John Moore had made her 1965 inaugural gown, which the First Lady described as "elegant, regal." Roxane Kaminstein, the designer for Samuel Winston, made the "white satin dress with the sparkly top" Mrs. Johnson wore to the inaugural gala, and rewore on several occasions, including the State Dinners in honor of the president of Pakistan and the prime minister of Italy in 1965 and the emperor of Ethiopia in 1967.[5] George Stavropoulos dressed her for her official White House portrait by Elizabeth Shoumatoff, which was in progress at the time of the fashion show, as well as making many of her gala gowns. Mollie Parnis and Adele Simpson provided the efficient little dresses, suits, and dress-and-jacket ensembles that made up the First Lady's working wardrobe, as well as some gowns.

The point of the show was to showcase American design, and all of the designers represented worked in the United States. However, some had foreign roots, passports, and accents. Pauline Trigère had been born in France to Russian émigrés, Rudi Gernreich in Austria. Both were Jews who came to America fleeing the Nazis; both were granted citizenship in the 1940s. Luba Marks was born in Bulgaria but raised in France; her parents were refugees of the Russian Revolution. Abe Schrader was born near Warsaw "and never quite lost his Polish accent" after immigrating to

George Stavro-poulos greets the Johnsons on a visit to the White House in the 1960s. (Courtesy Peter Stavropoulos)

In 1968, Mrs. Johnson chose a George Stavropoulos gown for her official portrait by Elizabeth Shoumatoff and sent the designer a framed print inscribed: "With appreciation for your artistry and friendship." (White House Collection/White House Historical Association)

the United States at age 20, with every intention of becoming a rabbi rather than an apparel manufacturer.[6] George Stavropoulos had been a successful designer in his native Greece before marrying an American who worked for the US embassy in Athens and moving to New York in 1961; he had not yet obtained US citizenship. Oscar de la Renta, who hailed from the Dominican Republic, would not become a citizen until 1971. Fernando Sarmi was an American citizen, but he was known as Count Sarmi in his native Italy. Adolfo was born Adolfo Sardiña in Cárdenas, Cuba; he immigrated to the United States as a teenager. So did London-born shoe designer David Evins, who served with the US Signal Corps in World War II. Clearly, the committee's definition of *American* was expansive. "The

designers themselves represented a melting pot of American fashion," the *Washington Post* explained: "the native born and the naturalized citizen."[7]

At the same time, a number of prominent American designers were excluded from the seemingly exhaustive list of participants. Early drafts of the guest list included the likes of Georgia Bullock, Charles Cooper, Chuck Geiger, Kimberly Kurts, Suzy Peretti, Richard Tam, Charles Kleibacker, Jo Copeland, Victor Joris, Leo Narducci, and Betsey Johnson; not one received an invitation, possibly because their clothes were not selected for the runway. On one early guest list, both Harvey Berin and Teal Traina (spelled "Trainer") are marked "no." Next to Berin's name, someone wrote: "follower—not a leader." Yet Berin and Traina both made the final cut.

In some cases, there is an explanation for the omission. Ben Zuckerman, whose firm made Mrs. Johnson's 1961 inaugural suit as well as clothes for Jackie Kennedy, had retired, as had Sally Victor, who sometimes made hats for the First Lady. Halston, who made Kennedy's pillbox hat for the 1961 inauguration ceremony, would not unveil his first ready-to-wear line until 1969. Oleg Cassini, Kennedy's "Secretary of Style," had closed his dress business after the assassination to focus on menswear and licensing. Arnold Scaasi, Sophie Gimbel, and Georgetown-based Charles Dunham—all of whom had dressed Mrs. Johnson—specialized in made-to-order clothing, not ready-to-wear. (Also, though based in New York, Scaasi was Canadian.) Bonnie Cashin, Vera Maxwell, and Norman Norell were invited to the show, but they were not represented on the runway; their pieces may have been cut after they sent their regrets (Norell was spending the winter in Palm Beach).[8] But other omissions are more perplexing. Helga Oppenheimer, Lilli Ann, and Dallas-based Justin McCarty were regularly featured in *Harper's*. And Mrs. Kennedy had helped propel her former classmate Lilly Pulitzer to fame in the early '60s; Happy Rockefeller was also a fan of Pulitzer's preppy prints.

The role of the fashion designer was in flux in America in the late 1960s. While haute couture, the highly regulated Parisian custom-made clothing industry, had long been driven by the creativity and personalities of individual designers—Worth, Poiret, Chanel, Lanvin, Dior—Seventh Avenue was historically dominated by faceless manufacturing firms who produced several ready-to-wear lines at various price points for shops across the country. Most prided themselves on the impressive volume of their output rather than its quality or originality. Even high-end manufacturers peddled authorized knockoffs of Parisian couture, not original designs. (As First Lady, Jacqueline Kennedy indulged her unpatriotic passion for French fashion by wearing licensed, line-for-line copies of Chanel suits, complete with Chanel fabric, trim, and buttons, made in the USA by New York's Chez Ninon.)

While the figureheads of these fashion factories arrived at work in chauffeured Cadillacs, their designers worked behind the scenes, their names known to industry insiders but rarely advertised.[9] Today, it is common practice for a designer to put his or her name on the label; this was a relatively new concept in 1968. It was more usual for the firm's (male) owner to put his name on the label, while the designer or designers—often female—toiled anonymously in the workroom. Thus, the Harvey Berin label was designed by Karen Stark; Malcolm Starr by Elinor Simmons; Abe Schrader by Belle Saunders; Jerry Silverman by Shannon B. Rodgers; and Teal Traina by Dominic Rompallo (who had replaced Chester Weinberg, who had replaced Geoffrey Beene). Stan Herman, still working today, designed the Mr. Mort label. Often, department stores replaced or augmented the manufacturers' labels with their own, further obscuring a garment's origins.

Designers might contract themselves to specialist or mass-market manufacturers on a temporary or freelance basis; thus, the White House fashion show featured "Don Simonelli for Modelia"; "Luba Marks for Elite Juniors"; and "Bill Blass for Bond Street," a luxury coat manufacturer, as well as "Bill Blass for Maurice Rentner." While a designer might change jobs frequently—adapting his or her style to each new position—a company's owner, name, and signature look remained consistent.

In the 1960s, however, designers increasingly made the transition from the creative to the business side, from the workroom to the front office.

Mr. Mort designer Stan Herman in a 1968 publicity photo (Author's collection)

Their names began to appear in small print at the bottom of labels; their faces began to appear in advertisements. Finally, they emerged from the shadows into the harsh glare of publicity. Geoffrey Beene launched his own label in 1963, followed by Donald Brooks in 1965. Bill Blass took over Maurice Rentner in 1970, renaming it Bill Blass Ltd. The Three Bs of Seventh Avenue represented not just a new business model but a new degree of familiarity accorded to designers that would have been unusual just 10 years earlier, when most worked for large manufacturers. In the 1950s, only "a small world of debutantes and editors took an interest in designers," Blass remembered in his autobiography, *Bare Blass*. "We were backroom boys in the grubby business to end all grubby businesses—Seventh Avenue."[10] By 1968, fashion designers could be brand names in their own right.

In 1969, Bernadine Morris would hail the designer's shift from hired hand to figurehead as "a turning point in American design" that had "not only lead to structural changes in the dress business but also produced a new attitude toward fashion."[11] But if these pioneering designer-businessmen reveled in their newfound freedom to design whatever they wanted rather than being constrained by a generic house style, they also had to worry about the bottom line for the first time. Their highly personal fashion statements needed to be wearable, or at least marketable.

And designers had to become not just salesmen but celebrities. Press Week, trunk shows, personal appearances, charity fashion shows, and high-profile society events across the country became part of the designer's rapidly expanding responsibilities. As Oscar de la Renta pointed out, "fame in New York doesn't mean fame in America. . . . We do masses of trunk shows, and if there was a charity event, a luncheon, or a black tie affair, I would go to it."[12] Like Parisian couture, American fashion was now fueled by the cult of personality. Designers were beginning to narrate their own runway shows, socialize with their well-heeled clients, and appear in magazine features, advertisements, and gossip columns. The White House fashion show was not just an honor, then, but an opportunity for the designers to cultivate their personal brands.

The audience had a different perspective. Mrs. Johnson had noted that fashion shows of the 1950s and '60s typically featured a celebrity table.[13] At the White House fashion show, the designers were the celebrities. "To add spice to the occasion, there was a designer or two at every table," Wauhillau La Hay reported.[14] (The designers also added some testosterone to the occasion, as most of them were men.) Great care was taken with the seating arrangements, especially for the First Lady's table. ("Bess always chooses such a delightful table for me," Mrs. Johnson once remarked.)[15] Abell sent Mrs. Johnson an annotated list for her approval, describing her tablemate Pauline Trigère as "charming, bright and entertaining"; Nat Bader, president of the coat company Originala, as a "delightful man"; and Oscar de la Renta as a "charming, delightful young designer—you will like him."[16] Trigère, in return, praised Mrs. Johnson: "I think she's the most charming woman I ever met."[17] They joined Nancy White, Eugenia Sheppard ("who can act as sort of a pool"), and the wives of the governors of Massachusetts, Vermont, North Dakota, Arkansas, and Maine.[18] Rudi Gernreich was seated right on the runway, at Lynda Robb's table. The "young and handsome" Nancy Trowbridge, wife of the secretary of commerce, was with Kasper and Jeanne Campbell. "Exotic, elegant" Aida Gardner—wife of the secretary of health, education, and welfare—sat with David Evins and Don Simonelli.[19]

Rudi Gernreich wore this Pierre Cardin Nehru jacket to the White House. (Courtesy of the FIDM Museum at the Fashion Institute of Design & Merchandising, Los Angeles, CA, Rudi Gernreich Archive, Bequest of the Rudi Gernreich Estate)

"It was obvious that the designers and politicians' wives enjoyed their meeting of two different worlds," the *New York Times* observed. "Mrs. Ralph M. Paiewonsky, wife of the governor of the Virgin Islands, told David Evins, the shoe designer, that she would swap her homemade mango chutney for a pair of his shoes. He told her to write down her size."[20] Nonetheless, many of the designers were strangers to the women in the audience; at a time when fashion designers still operated in relative anonymity, even those who wore their clothes did not necessarily know what they looked like. Mrs. Spiro Agnew, wearing a gray suit with royal blue trim, and Mrs. John Bell Williams, wife of the governor of Mississippi, asked Eleni Epstein to point out her favorite designers to them.[21]

In some cases, it was self-evident, as "the clothes the designers wore added an exotic note to the conservative choices of the governors' ladies." Designer Pauline Trigère wore her trademark tortoise-rimmed glasses, plastic shoes, and a sleeveless red wool dress of her own design with a gold turtle pinned to her hem.[22] (She collected turtles, the Chinese symbol of longevity and luck.)[23] Sportswear designer Jeanne Campbell (of Sportwhirl) appeared in a black silk micro-miniskirt and frilly white blouse with boots and a black fur handbag.[24] Gernreich, who'd flown in from Los Angeles, "caused big stir" in a "far-out costume" of navy blue Pierre Cardin Nehru jacket with gold buttons, white turtleneck, and camel-colored trousers.[25] The jacket survives in Gernreich's archive at the Fashion Institute of Design and Merchandising Museum and Galleries. "I think I'm the only tieless man in the room," Gernreich quipped.[26] Bill Blass also had "a closet full of the French designer's clothes," telling the *New York Times* in 1967: "If there's anyone who's had influence on American men's fashion, it's Cardin."[27]

Many of the American designers and manufacturers represented in the show were household names in 1968, though they are forgotten today. The selection reflected the organizers' desire to include a wide range of industry stalwarts and buzzy newcomers, representing multiple price points and healthy balance of the wearable and the weird. The Three Bs were at the top of the Seventh Avenue pyramid. Just below them, James Galanos, Chester Weinberg, and Rudi Gernreich were cult favorites and critical darlings. Adele Simpson, Pauline Trigère, and Mollie Parnis were long-established purveyors of crisp, classic femininity. John Moore and George Stavropoulos were famous for making dramatic gowns for the First Lady, among other illustrious clients. Oscar de la Renta was a relative newcomer; he had presented his first solo collection in 1965. B. H. Wragge was be-

Bill Blass, dubbed America's "King of Fashion" by President Gerald Ford, in 1966 (Photofest)

loved by Lynda Robb and her generation. Malcolm Starr was, according to Nina Hyde, "the savior of Washington since his evening dresses sell for only about $200 and they have a good but safe look."[28] The unwritten hierarchy of Seventh Avenue circa 1968 is suggested by the number of outfits allotted to each designer in the fashion show. While the majority were represented by just one or, occasionally, two outfits, a select few among the upper echelons had three or four. Only Blass got five.

President Gerald Ford would introduce Bill Blass to Queen Elizabeth II as America's "King of Fashion."[29] Blass revolutionized American sportswear, effortlessly blending Hollywood glamour with no-nonsense modernism. Blass dressed socialites and celebrities in elegant, effortless clothes appropriate for charity galas and country club luncheons. "Tanned and healthy, with bright blue eyes, bright white teeth, and a vague resemblance to Burt Lancaster," Blass was one of the first American designers to move in the same circles as his moneyed clients, making regular appearances in the society pages.[30] He wore Savile Row suits and amassed a collection of art and antiquities, much of which he left to the Metropolitan Museum of Art.

Blass was born and raised in Indiana; his mother was a dressmaker. He earned enough money sketching evening gowns for a Seventh Avenue manufacturer to put himself through Parsons School of Design.[31] But his promising career was interrupted by World War II. Blass enlisted in the army, where he was assigned to the 603rd Camouflage Battalion, or the "Ghost Army." His design training helped him create inflatable tanks, dummy camps, and other visual and audio diversions to confuse the enemy. Returning to New York in 1945, he worked behind the scenes for several major garment manufacturers before launching his own label.

The next best-represented designer, with four garments, was also one of the youngest: 35-year-old Oscar de la Renta. De la Renta, who died in 2014, is remembered for creating elegant, feminine evening gowns for socialites, celebrities, and First Ladies from Jacqueline Kennedy to Michelle Obama. But long before he ruled the red carpet, de la Renta was the cool new kid in town, designing Day-Glo miniskirts and fur-trimmed tunics for '60s jet-setters. With a Russian-inspired fall collection, he received his first Coty Award in 1967; he would be awarded his second in 1968.

Oscar de la Renta (*left*) with his wife, *Vogue* editor Françoise de Langlade, and Count Vega del Ren in the Bahamas on August 1, 1968 (Rue des Archives/ Granger, NYC)

Born Oscar Renta in the Dominican Republic, de la Renta left home as a teenager to study painting in Spain. He began sketching for fashion houses to make extra money and landed an apprenticeship with the legendary Cristóbal Balenciaga. By 1961, he was in Paris, working for the house of Lanvin. Eager to try his hand at ready-to-wear, de la Renta turned down a job with Christian Dior and moved to New York in 1963. "He had become Oscar 'de la' Renta somewhere between Paris and New York," joked James Brady, the publisher of *Women's Wear Daily*. "I had to assume that the aristocratic 'de la' had been handed out on the Pam Am jet along with the plastic tray and the Rock Cornish game hen."[32] But the moniker suited his aristocratic good looks and courtly manners. He began designing for Elizabeth Arden and Jane Derby; he bought the Jane Derby company in 1965 and relaunched under his own name. In 1967, he married French *Vogue* editor Françoise de Langlade. A few months after his appearance in the White House fashion show, *Vogue* would publish a picture of the dashing young designer, shirtless, water-skiing in the Bahamas alongside the Cushing sisters and Contessa Consuelo Crespi under the headline "The Beautiful People."[33]

Adolfo was one of those who sent his regrets; he was already committed to making a store appearance that day. After the show, he sent the First Lady a note of apology, along with a gift: a custom-made hat. She replied, "You were very much missed at the Fashion Show Luncheon—I am *so* sorry it was not possible for you to be with us."[34] Adolfo had made the red velour hat Mrs. Johnson wore to the 1965 inaugural ceremony along with a Sophie Gimbel coat and dress, and he continued to make hats for her thereafter.[35] Just as the Three Bs had fought for their financial and artistic freedom, Adolfo had left the hat company Emme, where he was head designer, to launch his own namesake label in 1963, using a $10,000 loan from Blass. (He was so successful that he repaid it within six months.) Though best known as a milliner, he was becoming increasingly recognized for his richly embellished clothing designs; he had apprenticed with Balenciaga and Chanel, and at the time of the fashion show he regularly dressed luminaries like the Duchess of Windsor, Babe Paley, Betsy Bloomingdale, and Nancy Reagan. But he firmly believed, "It's a designer's duty to take care of the size four as well as the size eighteen woman."[36] In 1969, Adolfo would win a Coty Award for his clothing designs to go along with the two he had already received for his millinery.

James Galanos photographed in his Los Angeles studio on April 1, 1965, with a model wearing his white and navy lace evening coat (George Brich, Valley Times Collection/Los Angeles Public Library)

James Galanos, who had also dressed the First Lady, was a no-show, too; he was away on a trip to Europe. Born James Gorgoliatos to Greek immigrants in Philadelphia, Galanos apprenticed with the Paris couturier Robert Piguet. He brought couture techniques and luxurious European fabrics back with him to America, with corresponding price tags; his clothes were said to be impossible to copy, because they were so intricately made. As his house model Pud Gadiot put it: "He brings almost a reverence to his work and he demands the same from the people he works with. He won't accept anything second rate."[37] At the time, Los Angeles was just coming into its own as a fashion capital. The country's second-largest apparel market was best known for mass-producing inexpensive sportswear and swimwear, but an emerging group of serious designers was lured west by the chance to run their own businesses outside the Seventh Avenue establishment. Galanos opened his business there in 1951; Austrian-born Rudi Gernreich, and Gustave Tassell, a native Philadelphian, followed. (Tassell had dressed Mrs. Johnson's predecessor, Jackie Kennedy, most famously making the dress she wore to ride an elephant in Jaipur in 1962.) In 1964, Mrs. Johnson wore a yellow wool dress and matching coat by Galanos that she considered her "best clothes."[38] But she did not wear Galanos often; he was too expensive. That did not deter Nancy Reagan, who remained a faithful Galanos client until he retired in 1998.

The First Lady also longed for clothes from Marquise, owned by Walter Croen but designed by Christian Mann. In 1967, after Croen showed her "several ensembles" during a shopping session at the Waldorf Hotel in New York, she confessed: "For the last three years one or two of his dresses or costumes had been a backbone of my wardrobe. But I can't afford many. I yearned for several." Mann's ladylike, matchy-matchy suits and dress-and-coat ensembles suited the First Lady's style and lifestyle; when she called them "useful," she meant the word as high praise. A few days before the fashion show, on February 15, Mrs. Johnson bought a yellow cotton Marquise suit from the spring collection in New York "and yearned for two more, but they're so expensive and I get scared when I count up the prices."[39] The collection would be Mann's last for the Marquise label; appropriately, he was hired away by another of the First Lady's favorites, Adele Simpson.

Stanley Marcus introduced Mrs. Johnson to Simpson around the time of Kennedy's inauguration. He called her "a middle-of-the-road designer" known for her "feminine and flattering" clothes.[40] Mrs. Johnson would remain a loyal Simpson client for years; her clothes were particularly suited to the First Lady's "shorter, petite figure."[41] (At 4'9", the designer herself was so petite that she had to stand on a box to narrate her fashion shows.) The youngest of five sisters, Simpson landed her first Seventh Avenue job at the age of 17, having performed in vaudeville as a child. In 1945—long before the Three Bs launched their namesake labels—Simpson bought the firm she designed for, Mary Lee Inc., and gave it her own name.[42] She won a Coty Award in 1947; by the time she met Mrs. Johnson, however, her clothes were decidedly conservative, if sophisticated and responsive to trends. "Adele Simpson's dresses are security blankets for scores of women around the country who know she will never embarrass them by putting her label on a dress that is bizarre," Bernadine Morris wrote. "Her clothes are known as sure sellers—on the fashion beat, but never ahead of it."[43]

Simpson never sketched; rather, she worked directly with fabrics—some she designed herself, others she sourced on her travels to India, China, and South America. She introduced cotton and sari fabric for eveningwear, adding an unconventional textile twist to her conservative silhouettes. She was also a frequent visitor to Paris, where she drew inspiration from haute couture and adapted it for American lifestyles. At a time when many of Seventh Avenue's top designers were men, Simpson claimed to understand women's needs better than her male competitors did. Her typical customer was "busy with charity work if she doesn't have a job. She doesn't take hours to get dressed. She has no maid to take care of her wardrobe, and she travels a lot."[44] Simpson specialized in streamlined, coordinated dress-and-jacket combinations, which could go from day to evening with minimal fuss. Just a few weeks before the White House fashion show, on February 8, the First Lady wore a champagne satin Simpson gown to a dinner for the British prime minister, Harold Wilson, in the State Dining Room.

Simpson's rival, Mollie Parnis, had a long history with the First Lady, dating back to the early days of LBJ's vice presidency, when Mrs. Johnson attended a Parnis trunk show at Neiman Marcus in Dallas. But the two women formed a close working relationship in the summer of 1964. "She really needed help," Parnis remembered. "Particularly under those circumstances."[45] The "circumstances," of course, were her new and unlooked-for duties as First Lady in the aftermath of President Kennedy's assassination. Parnis wrote and offered her services "to you and your daughters in the massive adjustment in your public life which will automatically bring up many clothing problems. I had the honor of designing most of Mrs. Eisenhower's clothes and also those of Margaret Truman. Therefore I know my way in the maze of planning an official wardrobe."[46] Bess Abell accepted on the First Lady's behalf.

"I'm not interested in designing for the average housewife," Parnis told *LIFE* magazine. "I don't even know her." Dressing the First Lady made her "feel I am part of history," she said. "I have never gone into the White House when my heart has not skipped several beats. The first time President Eisenhower called me Mollie, I thought I'd die."[47] Parnis didn't set trends or follow them. She "makes pretty dresses for women who are more concerned with showing off a graceful neck or waistline than they are with keeping up with the latest vagaries of fashion," as Bernadine Morris diplomatically put it.[48] Indeed, Parnis encouraged her clients to wear their dresses for years rather than replacing them every season—a strategy that appealed to the frugal First Lady. Mrs. Johnson's favorite dress—white with a beaded jacket—was by Parnis. She described another Parnis gown as "the sort of thing that I would leave to the Smithsonian and be proud of." In 1966, Mrs. Johnson wore a sequined and beaded green chiffon gown and shawl by Parnis to the State Dinner for Prime Minister Indira Gandhi of India. Her choice of a female designer was especially appropriate, as it was the first White House State Dinner honoring a female head of state. "If one did it well, one could make a career of dressing for this job!" Mrs. Johnson remarked in her diary that evening, at the end of "a day alive with drama."[49]

At the State Dinner for Indira Gandhi on March 28, 1966, Lady Bird admired the prime minister's "dark purple sari, very elegant, with a big gold-leaf design," as she described it in her diary. (LBJ Library photo by Frank Wolfe)

The president frequently turned to Parnis when he wanted to buy dresses for his wife or female friends. "I think the President had an idea that I owned all the dress houses in New York City," Parnis once said. "I am sure it never occurred to him that I only occupied one floor in this building and only employed about a hundred and fifty people . . . because very often he would ask me for things that I didn't make. I would usually get them for him." She even made the president some shirts once, though she'd never done menswear before, and embroidered some slippers for him. "I had a feeling that most of the people that were around him only told him what he wanted to hear, and that one of the contributions that I made to his life was that I really told it to him the way it was," she explained. But she appreciated that it was the president who had the final say on his wife's

wardrobe, despite Mrs. Johnson's "very definite ideas" and "innately good taste."[50] On February 13, just days before the fashion show, Mrs. Johnson reflected in her diary: "There are at least two women from the world of fashion that I've come to think of as my very special friends, Adele Simpson and Mollie Parnis."[51]

Marylin Bender described Larry Aldrich as "a taciturn dress manufacturer who plainly longed to be a scholar" and "actually succeeded in becoming a connoisseur and patron," amassing a collection of Monets, Matisses, and Picassos.[52] Aldrich became acquainted with the First Lady as a member of the American Federation of the Arts, a group of fine arts collectors who visited the White House for tea and a tour in November 1967. The First Lady was actively seeking donations to the White House collection and may have hoped he would contribute something from his collection. "Larry Aldrich talked with me about Lynda and her taste in clothes—excellent he thought," she wrote in her diary.[53] (Praising Lynda was a surefire way into her good graces.) But Aldrich was not a designer; the Larry Aldrich label was designed by Marie McCarthy, who had a talent for translating trends into wearable and affordable clothing.[54] Both were invited to the show, though neither attended; Mozella Roberts modeled an Aldrich dress on the runway.

On the "weird" end of the spectrum was Rudi Gernreich, who had secured his place in the fashion history books with his topless "monokini" bathing suit of 1964. His controversial clothes were body-conscious with a theatrical flair, testifying to his training in modern dance. (A career in

Left: The First Lady chose a Mollie Parnis gown and matching shawl of green chiffon for the State Dinner for Prime Minister Indira Gandhi. (Courtesy of the Museum of Texas Tech University)

Right: Mrs. Johnson often requested alterations to the sketches Mollie Parnis presented her, dropping hemlines or removing belts, but this one was left relatively intact. (LBJ Library)

dance was a surprisingly common prerequisite for fashion designers at the time. Luba Marks had been a member of the Ballet Russe de Monte Carlo; Vera Maxwell had danced with the Metropolitan Opera corps de ballet; Kasper had been a chorus boy.)[55] In 1967, Gernreich told the *New York Times:* "Fashion has become play acting, spoofing, wild, and charming. A woman can look like anything she wants—a schoolboy, a kindergartner, a gangster."[56] Both his fans and his critics agreed that his clothes—with their psychedelic colors, op art patterns, and futuristic silhouettes—were more costume than fashion. Three months before the fashion show, on December 1, 1967, Gernreich had appeared on the cover of *Time* magazine, flanked by two models in his peekaboo minidresses. By that time, Gernreich had already won three Coty Awards and been inducted into the Hall of Fame. (The Coty Awards functioned in much the same way as the Best Dressed List, with repeat winners eventually being canonized and removed from the annual competition.)

George Stavropoulos made his name with diaphanous draped evening-wear imitating the classical statuary of his native Greece. His distinctive gowns were modeled after togas, with layers, pleats, and floating panels in diaphanous chiffon, organza, and silk crepe, often in white and ivory; he was both behind and ahead of his times in his insistence on using natural fibers. Sensual but never bare, his gowns were wearable interpretations of the ethnic fashion fad. Stavropoulos's loyal customers—who included Elizabeth Taylor and Maria Callas as well as Mrs. Johnson—defended his high prices on the grounds that his clothes never went out of style.[57] They accessorized them with capes rather than tailored coats and simple, classically inspired hairstyles and jewelry.

Mrs. Johnson adored his "lovely chiffon evening dresses" and once said that wearing one "would make a clod feel like a lady." In 1967, she had purchased his "exquisite yellow chiffon that looks like a Botticelli girl dancing in the dell, scattered with little daisies down the front," wearing it to the State Dinner in honor of the prime minister of Thailand on May 8, 1968. In November 1968, Stavropoulos would be the only fashion designer the First Lady invited to "the biggest, the best, the favorite party" on the White House social calendar, for the National Council on the Arts.[58] A contemporary profile of the designer revealed: "When not poring over those crepes and silk jerseys that he fashions into seductive and sophisticated evening clothes, Stavropoulos enjoys painting in oils and reading plays by Tennessee Williams."[59] With his dark, curly hair and exotic accent, he resembled actor Ricardo Montalbán; a wealthy client once offered his wife a million dollars to divorce him.[60]

Though jewelry designer Kenneth Jay Lane was not mentioned in Nancy White's remarks, he (with his staff of 200) must have provided the lion's share of the accessories, for he was the only jeweler to receive an invitation to the show. Many of the models wore the enormous, Indian-inspired door knocker earrings so popular at the time (popular with everyone except the First Lady, that is). Lane had started the trend; a former a shoe designer for Christian Dior, he had developed a method of attaching rhinestones without weighing down the shoe, which he adapted to oversized earrings.[61] Lane's "real jewelry in unreal materials" earned him a Special Coty Award in 1966 and helped make costume jewelry acceptable among those who

Lady Bird wore her "Botticelli girl" dress by George Stavropoulos to the State Dinner in honor of the prime minister of Thailand on May 8, 1968. (LBJ Library photo by Robert Knudsen)

could afford the real thing. Bess Abell went on a shopping spree at Lane's New York showroom with Nina Hyde in early January 1968, while the Johnsons were spending the holidays at their Texas ranch. "Not since I was a child into my Mother's paint and powder and jewelery have I had such a good time," Abell wrote to Lane. "Thank you for letting Nina Hyde and me descend on you, your show room and stock rooms. It was glorious fun! And, yesterday I got a new dress to match the earrings." Privately, she wished she'd bought the matching necklace and bracelet too.[62]

David Evins attended the show, though he was not credited in the narration; the elder statesman of the American shoe industry likely provided the majority of the shoes for the show, although Bill Blass and Beth Levine also sent some shoes and boots. Evins had already worked with many of the designers involved—including Blass, Beene, Parnis, Galanos, Tassell, and de la Renta—on their Press Week shows; his wife, Marilyn, was a loyal Galanos client.[63] Evins called fashion shows "a labor of love" because many designers "didn't have the money" to buy shoes for their models.[64] Nicknamed the "King of Pumps," Evins was known for his lightweight, comfortable pumps with flattering, low-cut profiles. His celebrity clients included Judy Garland, Marilyn Monroe, and Ava Gardner; he made Grace Kelly's wedding shoes. More importantly, his shoes were worn by Mamie Eisenhower, Jaqueline Kennedy, and Mrs. Johnson, who had worn his satin pumps to Luci's wedding; he would dress every subsequent First Lady through the Reagan administration.

Born in Ohio, George Halley milked cows on his family's farm until he graduated from high school, then hitchhiked to New York to follow his dream of becoming a fashion designer. He began his career as a window dresser at Lord & Taylor; designer Charles James admired his work and gave him a job in his atelier. In 1958, he married Claudia Morgan, a model for Norman Norell, who became his muse, model, and sometime salesgirl; Norell designed the wedding gown and gave the bride away. "I never design anything Claudia wouldn't wear," Halley once said. When LBJ visited Norell's showroom in 1963, the then vice president met Morgan and told her: "Claudia—that is really Ladybird's name. I bet you didn't know that."[65]

Halley worked his way up in the business, getting fired by Jo Copeland before launching his own line in 1967. He was the rare Seventh Avenue designer who could construct a garment from start to finish; he always made one or two dresses in each collection himself, "just for luck."[66] He'd made headlines by banning false eyelashes from his spring 1968 show, fearing that they would clash with his gauzy, high-waisted, antebellum-style "Tara dresses," inspired by "that Southern girl I'm married to," he joked; Claudia hailed from Durham, North Carolina. "They look like femininity unleashed," Bernadine Morris gushed.[67] Despite their "astronomical" prices in the "$600 to $3000" range, his dance-floor-friendly gowns appealed to "rich ladies who want beautiful clothes that are structured impeccably" as well as celebrities like Dionne Warwick.[68]

Named for the 70-carat Kimberley Diamond, the Kimberly knitwear company was known as "the Rolls Royce of the knitwear industry"—a description the company's car-collecting founder, Jack Lazar, must have appreciated. When Lazar launched the company in 1946, after serving in the army during World War II, knitwear had fallen on hard times. Many women refused to buy knits because of their propensity to stretch, sag, and shrink. But Lazar was not afraid to experiment with sturdy novelty yarns and synthetics, and he always emphasized fashion as well as quality, trekking to Paris for the couture

George Halley with his wife and muse, Claudia, wearing his navy tulle dress, in a 1967 publicity photo (Author's collection)

shows to keep abreast of trends. Slowly, Kimberly led the knitwear industry away from the hand-knitted look and into flat, lightweight double knits. "Jazzier styling, brighter colors and new blends are making converts out of women who might not have bought knitted suits, dresses and ensembles as well as shells for spring in past years"—including Kimberly clients like the Duchess of Windsor, Barbara Walters, and Mrs. Kennedy, who favored the company's Chanel-style unstructured knit suits. Barbra Streisand modeled color-blocked Kimberly dresses paired with white go-go boots for *Vogue* in August 1965.[69] For 1968, the company introduced pantsuits, previously unheard of in knitwear. By 1969, Kimberly would be one of the largest privately owned clothing manufacturing companies in the United States, with annual sales of $30 million.

Born in Paris to a tailor and a dressmaker, Pauline Trigère was destined for a career in fashion. Her first job was as a trainee cutter for the haute couture house Martial et Armand. But Hitler's rise convinced Trigère, who was Jewish, to leave France with her young family. They arrived in New York on the SS *Normandie* in 1937. "We had planned to stop in New York only briefly on our way to Chile, but we took a double-decker bus ride from 57th Street to 34th Street," Trigère recalled decades later. "On the way, I got a look at the dummies in the store windows. They were showing copies of Paris dresses, and I knew I could do that—probably better."[70]

Trigère worked for Hattie Carnegie before opening her own Seventh Avenue fashion house in 1942, dressing clients like Claudette Colbert, Lena Horne, and the Duchess of Windsor. Eleni Epstein, who wore a lot of Trigère, called her "an intellectual designer, the designer's designer. Her clothes are so well assembled—with a sense of the body and movement underneath, and such a strong sense of shape—that function is never sacrificed for chic. In essence, Trigère has provided made-to-order couture for the wholesale market—not an easy accomplishment."[71] Trigère's clothes had a Parisian flair for the dramatic, featuring capes and fur borders; she only wore her own designs. She had been inducted into the Coty Award Hall of Fame in 1959. In 1968, she was still the only woman to have earned that honor besides Claire McCardell, who had received it posthumously.

You could take the designer out of Paris, but you couldn't take Paris out of the designer. A slight 5'4", with "a staccato accent that might remind you of a French machine gun" and a penchant for red lipstick, Trigère was almost a caricature of an imperious Frenchwoman.[72] Instead of sketching, she draped her designs using traditional couture techniques. Cut and fabric were more important to her than ornamentation; the *New York Times* called her designs "plain to the point of abstraction, but in a good way."[73] It was not Trigère's first visit to the White House; on that occasion, in 1962, she said: "I felt the same emotion when I visited the President's house for the first time as I did when I revisited Versailles."

Pauline Trigère leaving the White House in 1962 (Reprinted with permission of the DC Public Library, Star Collection © *Washington Post*)

Red, White, and Blue on the Runway

Jacques Tiffeau was French too. He trained with Dior and turned down the chance to take over the House of Dior after Yves Saint Laurent left (the job went to Marc Bohan). Instead, Tiffeau immigrated to the United States, where he embraced post–World War II synthetics and manufacturing techniques. His company, Tiffeau & Busch, offered young women less expensive versions of sophisticated silhouettes and daringly high miniskirts. A collector of Asian art, Tiffeau was an avowed minimalist, creating clothes that were clean, graphic, and sculptural. "The secret of good clothes is to keep taking off, simplifying, trimming down—yet to capture the shape of the human body," he once said. Renée Hunter, who worked as his house model, describes his style as "very simple, very clean. . . . He didn't like buttons so he used a lot of zippers." Tiffeau's clothes didn't need embellishment, because "he had great fabric sense and a great sense of color." But his moods could be dramatic; once, when Hunter arrived late to work, "he got pissed and locked the door."[74] His friend Robert Motherwell, the artist, described the temperamental and talented Frenchman as "like having a beautiful leopard in the room."[75]

Though John Moore had designed the First Lady's inaugural gown, the fashion show marked his first trip to the White House; the fittings for that gown had been done in New York. "It's a great honor to be here," he said.[76] After greeting Mrs. Johnson in the receiving line, he took his seat next to Happy Rockefeller, whose husband was expected to run for president on the Republican ticket that fall. "With things as they look right now in the Presidential sweepstakes, maybe John was trying to convince the New York Governor's wife that he could do a repeat performance," the *Philadelphia Inquirer* noted waspishly.[77]

Donald Brooks is today the least famous of the Three Bs, but he dressed the boldface names of his time: including Princess Grace, Barbra Streisand, Faye Dunaway, and Jacqueline Kennedy, who wore Brooks for her televised *Tour of the White House* in 1962. Mrs. Johnson was a fan, and Lynda Robb was also a faithful client; she had worn his beige minidress to meet Russian premier Aleksei Kosygin and his family at the Glassboro Summit Conference in 1967 and sent Brooks a picture from the event a few days after the fashion show.[78] One of the first American designers to

Mrs. Johnson greets John Moore, who designed her inaugural gown, in the receiving line before the fashion show; China Machado waits at far right. (*Chicago Daily News*)

Lynda Bird Johnson accompanied her parents to the 1967 Glassboro Summit Conference, wearing a Donald Brooks dress. (LBJ Library photo by Kevin Smith)

cross over into theater and film costuming, Brooks could not attend the show because he was in Hollywood designing Julie Andrews's wardrobe for *Darling Lili*.[79] (He would receive an Oscar nomination for her 1968 movie *Star!* for which he created more than 3,500 costumes.)

Though unknown today, Chester Weinberg was nearly as famous as Brooks, Beene, and Blass; his clothes would appear on the cover of *Vogue* in both March and April of 1968. Weinberg had worked with Harvey Berin and Jo Copeland before replacing Geoffrey Beene as the designer for Teal Traina. He followed in Beene's footsteps and launched his own label in 1966. By 1967, Marylin Bender noted, he was "moving swiftly along the trail blazed by Bill Blass."[80] A quotable favorite of the fashion press, Wein-

berg wore Savile Row suits and dressed socialites and celebrities, including "Baby" Jane Holzer, Judy Peabody, and Amanda Burden, Babe Paley's daughter. His prices had recently climbed, however, and his dresses now started at $89, on a par with Geoffrey Beene's. "Chester fans pine for the Chester that started out in the world of fashion with a much more reasonable tag," *Women's Wear Daily* noted just two weeks before the White House show, adding that some buyers found his prices too high for such youthful clothes.[81]

Herbert Kasper, a designer of remarkable versatility and longevity, was equally comfortable designing "better dresses" and sportswear, whether as the face of his own label or as a designer for Arnold & Fox

Herbert Kasper—better known as Kasper—in a 1967 publicity photo; he was represented by two polka-dotted ensembles on the runway. (Author's collection)

and Joan Leslie, a division of Leslie Fay. As a child, he made clothes for his sisters; during World War II, he enlisted in the army, where he created costumes for shows to entertain the troops. After the war, Kasper studied with Pauline Trigère at Parsons, then continued his fashion education in Paris, where he worked for Jacques Fath and Christian Dior. When he returned to New York in 1950, he was only 23; he won his first Coty Award in 1955.[82] He was admired for making expensive-looking clothes "of high quality a moderate price," a skill that endeared him to his most prominent client, Mrs. Johnson—but his designs were youthful and exciting enough to appeal to her daughter, Lynda, too.[83]

Like Kasper, Hollywood costume designer William Travilla usually went by his last name alone; he launched his eponymous ready-to-wear line, Travilla, in the early 1950s. Today, he is remembered for designing

the iconic pleated white halter dress Marilyn Monroe wore atop a subway grate in 1955's *The Seven Year Itch*. In February 1968, however, he was riding high on the success of *The Valley of the Dolls*, the film version of Jacqueline Susann's bestseller, released in December 1967. The sudsy showbiz tale was punctuated with fashion montages, and its stars—Patty Duke, Sharon Tate, and Barbara Parkins—wore trendy clothes in silhouettes similar to those Travilla showed on the White House runway.

Stella Sloat joined her family's sportswear firm, Sloat & Co., right out of high school. Unusually for a sportswear designer, she regularly traveled to Paris for inspiration and bought her fabrics in Europe. Her devotion to practical yet upscale clothing won her a seat on a task force of the President's

Committee for Employment of the Handicapped.[84] *Women's Wear Daily* dubbed her "The Skirt Queen" for bringing back separates at a time when dresses and suits ruled fashion. In 1970, Sloat would secure her place in American history by designing the uniform of the Girl Scouts.[85]

Harvey Berin had dressed Mamie Eisenhower, Bess Truman, and all three Johnson women, though Jackie Kennedy seems to have been turned off by his reputation as "follower—not a leader." Berin—or, rather, his designer, Karen Stark—strove to please "Fifth Avenue as well as Des Moines" with ladylike, conservative clothes in high-quality fabrics, at a time when many designers were chasing trends and experimenting with synthetics.[86]

Despite the tardy nature of the invitations, 27 of the designers and manufacturers invited to the fashion show accepted. On the morning of the event, however, disaster struck: 10 of those expected to attend had their flights grounded by fog in New York, throwing the carefully planned seating chart into disarray at the last possible moment.[87] The first entry in Lady Bird's official diary for the day is ominous: "Breakfast. Talked with Bess re guest list."[88] Geoffrey Beene, Adele Simpson, Oscar de La Renta, Nat Bader (of Originala), Fernando Sarmi, Anne Fogarty, Adri (Adrienne Steckling, who designed the sportswear label B. H. Wragge), Kenneth Jay Lane, Seymour Fox, and Luba Marks were left stranded, along with *Glamour* editor Ruth Whitney. Adolfo, James Galanos, Jacques Tiffeau, Bill Blass, Bonnie Cashin, Malcolm Starr, Abe Schrader, Larry Aldrich, Marie McCarthy, Norman Norell, and Donald Brooks had already sent their regrets, pleading prior commitments. Those who made it were Pauline Trigère, Chester Weinberg, John Moore, George Stavropoulos, Mollie Parnis, Walter Croen (of Marquise), William Travilla, David Evins, Harvey Berin, Kasper, Don Simonelli, Jerry Silverman, Jeanne Campbell (of Sportwhirl), Stella Sloat, Sidney Wragge (the Council of Fashion Designers of America's first president and the head of B. H. Wragge), and Rudi Gernreich.[89] While many newspapers printed the show's official guest list, it did not take the last-minute no-shows into account and cannot be relied upon. Most accounts also overreported the number of governors' wives, claiming that anywhere from 39 to 43 attended; in fact, many did not come to Washington with their husbands.

The unfortunate designers' desperate telegrams to the First Lady—preserved in the Johnson Presidential Library—make for heartbreaking reading. Luba Marks—who had been so surprised to receive an invitation that she called the White House to make sure it wasn't a joke—waited two hours for the fog to clear at La Guardia before dashing to Newark in hopes of getting a flight.[90] "Being completely frustrated and almost in tears I secretly wished that perhaps Superman himself might miraculously appear to whisk me to Washington under the folds of his cape," she wrote. "It is a great disappointment to me not to have had the opportunity and pleasure of meeting you. Some things unfortunately happen only once in a lifetime and I missed my once."[91] Adele Simpson consoled herself with a Bloody Mary and pastrami and eggs at Lou Siegel's.[92] "I'm so disappointed, but it's wonderful we're finally having a fashion show in the White House," she told a reporter via long distance.[93]

That very morning, the *Washington Post* reported that Adri "hasn't stopped shaking since she received her invitation." Breathlessly, the designer told the *Post*'s reporter: "I'm running through all my stock trying to find something to wear." She finally settled on a black and white printed silk, hoping "it would be proper." Instead, she was stuck in New York.[94]

However, the bad weather was a boon for behind-the-scenes players like Gillis MacGil, publicist Vera Gawanksy (Lambert's colleague, who represented Stavropoulos and other designers), and the *Harper's Bazaar* team, who were not originally on the guest list for the luncheon. Because of the high number of eleventh-hour cancellations, they all got seats in the audience. China Machado took Geoffrey Beene's place, Eve Orton filled in for Seymour Fox, Natalie Gittelson for Adri Steckling, and Gillis MacGil for Chester Weinberg, who, along with Mollie Parnis, was bumped to the head table, where they replaced Oscar de la Renta and Nat Bader. Gawanksy took Ruth Whitney's place next to Jeanne Campbell. Under Abell's clearheaded direction, tables for 10 became tables for eight; chairs, place settings, and menus were whisked away; and place cards discreetly rearranged. Everything was in place by 1:30, when the slightly less numerous guests, tipsy from cocktails in the East Foyer, made their way up the marble grand staircase, as the red-coated US Marine Band played all-American tunes in the rotunda.[95]

6

The Runway

As the "cruise director for the ship of state," Bess Abell was known for taking "great delight in giving old standby items on the menu new names. Like naming the dessert after the guest of honor or his wife."[1] Thus, while the nation's governors were being briefed by General Earle G. Wheeler at the State Department, their wives lunched on an all-American menu of "consommé White House," "chicken curry Columbus," green salad, and "Peppermint Boutique"—peppermint ice cream with chocolate sauce. "The President, who has had plenty of briefing from the general, walked out of that luncheon to greet the ladies."[2] LBJ's surprise appearance in the State Dining Room, just as the bespoke consommé was being served, drew a standing ovation from the designers in the room. The president "threaded his way between the 10 tables until he came to Lady Bird's table which was in the center under the portrait of Lincoln" and chatted with her tablemates. "There are so many governors running around here that I'm afraid to leave the place," he joked. "I'm afraid to pick up the telephone and find one of them answering it."[3] He stopped at Lynda's table to give her a kiss; on his way to the Red Room to greet the models, he kissed Happy Rockefeller so enthusiastically that her "Discover America" scarf fell off, and he shook hands with her tablemate, fellow Texan John Moore.[4]

"We were all wondering if we would get to meet President Johnson," Sherry Thomas said. "We were

The patriotic red, white, and blue luncheon menu featured "consommé White House" and "chicken curry Columbus." (LBJ Library)

Luncheon

*Krug
Gewürztraminer*   Consommé White House

Chicken Curry Columbus
Arbor Rice
Spring Greens

Peppermint Boutique

Demi-tasse

The White House
Thursday, February 29, 1968

all standing around . . . . and all of a sudden there was a little flurry and there he was!"[5] Peggy Parke was delighted to be one of a few models Bess Abell introduced to the president by name.[6] Denise Linden was another one. "Her husband [had been] in the military and he thanked her for his service," Lynda Hatch remembers. "He'd clearly been coached!" But Hatch was charmed nonetheless. "He was a much more attractive man than you might have thought from his photographs!" she says. "He was tall, he was in a beautifully tailored suit—he wasn't bad! He made a nice impression."[7] Even China Machado, who was "very anti-war," admitted that she was thrilled to meet the president.[8] Though Renée Hunter "was a JFK person," she says today: "When I look back at history at this point in my life, I realize that JFK had a plan, but LBJ made sure it happened."[9] But not all of the models were impressed. Thomas remembered:

> Several of the girls were very anti-Vietnam. My boyfriend had been in Vietnam. But I was in the White House! I was thrilled to be there. One of the models went way to the back because she didn't want to shake the president's hand. But I went right to the front and I was the first.
>
> My dad was a pilot in the war, and I once asked him, "What would you say if you met the president of the United States?" And he said: "Just say 'How do you do, Mr. President?'" I put out my hand and he took my hand and he had these big rancher hands. I'll never forget that! He didn't have those soft, weenie politician hands. And he said: "It's so nice to see so many pretty girls in the White House!" And I said in this little voice: "How do you do, Mr. President?"

Interviewed 50 years later, Thomas did a flawless LBJ impression. The president skipped the fashion show, telling the models he was going upstairs to take a nap—his standard post-lunch routine.[10] "Have a good show, girls," he said.[11]

Back in the State Dining Room, Mrs. Johnson put on her trusty reading glasses, tapped on her glass, and stood up to make her remarks.[12] Positioned directly under Lincoln's portrait, she began: "Welcome to the White House! I'm delighted you made it a stop on your 1968 travel agenda. Gathered in this room are some of the most accomplished tour guides in the country—the Governors' wives. I know because many of them have helped me discover their own states—from the white church steeples of covered bridges of New England to the wide open spaces of our Great American West." In her East Texas drawl, both "Governors'" and "West" had two syllables. She then turned her attention to the designers in the audience: "Since I have lived here I'm well aware of how fast a costume is out of date. . . . I must say—you ladies and gentlemen of the industry keep the present occupant busy with the hemline." She observed that the White House "in many ways mirrors fashion changes" and joked that "Mrs. Rutherford B. Hayes created a stir when she refused to go all out for the mod look of 1873—a bustle."[13] She concluded by introducing "an expert on both [fashion and travel]," *Harper's Bazaar* editor—and presidential appointee to the National Council on the Arts—Nancy White.[14]

From behind a podium at the foot of the runway, White—in a navy Geoffrey Beene coatdress with a white Bergdorf Goodman hat and a red carnation in her lapel—began her own remarks by thanking the First Lady.[15]

> Everyone involved in American fashion—in the art of it and in the economics of it—from designer to manufacturer, from store president to model—feels personal pride and boundless gratitude for the signal honor you have bestowed on us today.
>
> It is marvelous beyond words to realize that—although millions of people make the historic pilgrimage to Washington every year (and thousands, I am told, visit this house during the vacation season every day), today marks the very first time that fashion has come to the White House as an invited guest! Already the impact and the significance of this occasion has become the proud property of the whole world of fashion.

White promised a sartorial celebration of "all that is great and wonderful and exciting and everlasting in this land. . . . a sampling of the endemically, exuberantly American fashion that we expect will flower in every state of the Union this spring and summer."[16] Finally, the chandeliers dimmed, and the first of a series of "mood pictures"—the "Discover America" scarf—appeared on a swag-draped rear-projection screen behind the runway.[17] From the rotunda, the Marine Band struck up a John Philip Sousa march.

The half-hour presentation consisted of approximately 88 outfits by nearly 60 American designers and manufacturers; the exact number is

Left: Chaos reigned in the Blue Room as the models donned their first looks for the runway. (LBJ Library, White House Naval Photographic Unit, Outs Roll 15 of 16 of MP 893, *The President, February 1968*)

Right: Publicist Vera Gawansky, who worked with Eleanor Lambert, oversaw last-minute preparations in the Blue Room. (LBJ Library, White House Naval Photographic Unit, Outs Roll 15 of 16 of MP 893, *The President, February 1968*)

Mount Rushmore formed the back-drop to travel-ready outfits by Deanna Littell and White Stag. (LBJ Library photo by Robert Knudsen)

Lynda Hatch models a 1930s-style white jersey Travilla minidress in front of Old Faithful. (LBJ Library photo by Robert Knudsen)

difficult to pin down, because there is no complete visual or written record of the show, and several of the 100 ensembles trucked to Washington were cut from the packed schedule at the last minute. Even so, in order to fit them all in, several models had to share the runway at any given moment in. So brisk was the pace that one model missed her final turn on the runway. Each model wore three or four outfits, and they only had two minutes to change in the Blue Room before lining up in the Red Room to step back out onto the runway.[18] (The color symbolism of the rooms was "coincidence—they happened to be nearest the State Dining Room.")[19] While "everything moved smoothly out front to the soothing sounds of Nancy White's commentary," chaos reigned backstage.

Above left: Mozella Roberts wears a pink and pistachio minidress by Marie McCarthy for Larry Aldrich, showcased against a slide of San Francisco's Ghirardelli Square. (LBJ Library photo by Robert Knudsen)

Above right: The full skirt of Pauline Trigère's strapless white organdy dress with a back-buttoning bolero mirrored the dome of the Capitol. (LBJ Library photo by Robert Knudsen)

Left: Renée Hunter and Mozella Roberts model wash-and-wear Anne Fogarty in front of the Grand Canyon. (LBJ Library photo by Robert Knudsen)

Behind the runway, slides of American tourist destinations like the Grand Canyon, the Golden Gate Bridge, the Statue of Liberty, Old Faithful, and Mount Rushmore flashed on the rear-projection screen.[20] Ghirardelli Square, an abandoned San Francisco chocolate factory whose renovation and beautification into a public plaza and shopping center had made an impression on the First Lady during her California trip, was among the images.[21] The slides seem to have been coordinated to the dresses, so Pauline Trigère's bell-shaped white midi dress mirrored the dome of the Capitol Building, the bold prints of a trio of minidresses echoed the striations

Peggy Parke
models a white
chiffon gown with
iridescent jeweled
bodice by Mollie
Parnis against a
cherry blossom
backdrop. (LBJ
Library photo by
Robert Knudsen)

of the Grand Canyon, and the glittering New York City skyline seemed to reflect sparkly eveningwear. "That's like a Renoir," someone remarked of one flower-filled image.[22] The *Chicago Tribune* claimed that the 40-plus images projected behind the models were "Lady Bird's own slides," but the Department of the Interior actually supplied them.[23] The error is telling, however; the entire event was couched as a homespun affair born of the First Lady's patriotic love of America the Beautiful. It was emphatically *not* a flashy publicity gambit by big-city fashion editors and publicists.

Even the music reinforced the "Discover America" theme, with songs like "Chicago," "Oklahoma!," and "I Left My Heart in San Francisco" alternating with patriotic marches.[24] The Marine Band played so loudly that Mrs. Johnson scribbled four separate notes to Bess Abell asking that the music be toned down. But Eleanor Lambert disagreed: "That music is making the show!"[25]

"American style, you have to admit when you see a well selected cross-section, is something to discover," the *New York Post* mused. "The accent was on glamorous but practical, not kooky, clothes in fabrics that behave well, clothes to wear and enjoy." Major springtime trends included polka dots; opaque tights; printed dresses worn under jackets lined in the same fabric; bathrobe coats; frilly neo-Victorian shirts with high, lace-trimmed collars and puffy sleeves; belted everything; vests (or "sleeveless coats"); black and white; and, for evening, floor-length shirtdresses and floating chiffons and lace. The "youthquake" influence was visible in "jeune fille" or "babydoll" dresses with high waistlines and floral appliqués, ruffles, and smocking, and shrunken jackets, pleated skirts, and coats in schoolgirl tweeds. According to press reports, the prices ranged from $20 to well over $500.[26]

The so-called hemline wars spilled onto the runway, with minis, maxis, and the newly introduced midis battling for supremacy.[27] Bill Blass had it both ways, pairing a "very, very short" white lace minidress with a long linen coat—an ensemble "meant for evening in Palm Beach surroundings," Barbara Cloud hypothesized.[28] The mini had arrived in the United States from London in 1964 and quickly spread from nightclubs to college campuses and office buildings. Cynics predicted that the shocking style wouldn't outlast its first summer, but, as temperatures dropped, hemlines stayed put. Women determined to brave the cold in miniskirts simply added thick, colorful tights and boots. As historian Caroline Rennolds Milbank has pointed out, "the short skirt wasn't merely a hem length, it was a silhouette, characterized by a body-skimming fit with no accent on breasts, waist, or hips. . . . It was used for the simple, grown-up-but-youthful conservative style, for the mock-innocent baby-doll look, and for the wacky and with-it boutique designs."[29] The versatile mini endured for years, getting shorter and shorter along the way; first it bared the knees, then the lower thigh, then the entire leg. But as the 1960s spiraled into social and political chaos, skirts careened from thigh-high to floor-length and back. Sportswear designer Stella Sloat—dubbed "The Skirt Queen" by *Women's Wear Daily*—was, appropriately, represented on the runway by a ruffled plaid maxi skirt.

Amid this hemline hemming and hawing, the midi skirt emerged in 1967 as a chic and cerebral compromise. Today, the term *midi* is applied to knee-length skirts as often as tea-length skirts and pencil skirts as well as flowing A-lines. But it originally denoted a specific, unforgiving shape:

Countess-turned-model Yolande "Yoyo" d'Oultremont in a white linen officer's coat and lace-trimmed minidress by Bill Blass (LBJ Library photo by Robert Knudsen)

Left: An ankle-length dinner skirt in black and white plaid by Stella Sloat, dubbed "The Skirt Queen" (LBJ Library photo by Robert Knudsen)

Right: Jenny Chillcott models one of the few trouser ensembles on the runway, a white bush jacket and khaki pants by Ginori, accessorized with binoculars. (LBJ Library photo by Robert Knudsen)

Below: Red, white, and blue ensembles by Monte Sano, Kimberly, Roxane for Samuel Winston, and James Galanos opened the show (LBJ Library, White House Naval Photographic Unit, MP 893, *The President,* February 1968)

not mid-leg but mid-calf, widening from the waist to four inches below the knee. It was, and is, a tricky silhouette to pull off without looking stumpy or frumpy. With the wrong shoes, it was a disaster. While not as obviously youthful as the mini, it looked best on young, tall, slim women with the confidence to cover up. Chester Weinberg had been the first to show it on the runway; by 1968, it appeared in almost every American collection.[30] Donald Brooks didn't include a single full-length gown in his whole spring 1968 collection. "When night falls you can count on Donald for a Midi," *Women's Wear Daily* declared.[31] For Weinberg, the midi was "almost as a direct reflection of the women's movement. It's for those who don't particularly care about what men think about the way they dress."[32]

Pat Mori, modeling a red, white, and blue Originala coat of "spongy plaid tweed," with Helen Hite (in Monte Sano), Denise Linden (in Kimberly), Joan Pavlis (in Roxane for Samuel Winston), and Pud Gadiot (in James Galanos) (NARA)

Lynda Hatch, in a navy Seymour Fox coat and white Kimberly dress (LBJ Library photo by Robert Knudsen)

But for many men newly accustomed to seeing female legs on full display for the first time in history, it was an unwelcome step backward.

Designers (and shoppers) reluctant to commit to one length experimented with asymmetrical hemlines, handkerchief hemlines, culottes, knickers, gaucho pants, and long coats paired with short skirts. A *Vogue* headline of March 1968 declared, "Skirt Lengths: A Spring of Choice and Variety." In addition to the "sharp, modern, young" mini and the full-length or maxi skirt, there was the "witty and seductive" midi skirt, which "takes great dash to wear—and long beautiful legs that show well under the hem."[33] The *Boston Globe* suggested that Adele Simpson, a fan of the midi, should persuade her most famous client to wear it: "If the First Lady can 'put over' the look, anybody can. Everyone knows Mrs. Johnson isn't exactly the leggy type."[34] Some found fashion's infinite variety freeing; others were frustrated by the constantly changing rules, which seemed to mirror the restlessness of the times.

Though some of the spring 1968 collections included trousers—often so wide-legged that they could pass for skirts or paired with long coats or tunics that could double as dresses—women were still banned from wearing trousers in many restaurants and formal settings, and trouser ensembles were few and far between on the White House runway. Nancy White had also barred swimwear, explaining: "I felt we really shouldn't show any bathing suits in that room."[35]

The show was divided into four sections of about 20 looks each. Although numerous photos, contact sheets, and film clips documenting the event survive, as do White's script and notes, there is no definitive record of the looks shown on the runway. It is clear that some were dropped from the overstuffed lineup at the last minute or shown out of order. White's carefully typed and numbered script skips over some numbers and repeats others, suggesting eleventh-hour revisions. Some of the photos and film footage of the event were taken at the fittings and rehearsal and may not perfectly reflect what the governors' wives saw. It is likely that accessories and even models were swapped around on the fly; most of the Mannequin models were the same size, and their arsenal of wigs, hairpieces, and hats makes it difficult to distinguish individual models in many of the photos. (Today, even they can't tell themselves apart with absolute certainty). The following account is pieced together from multiple visual and documentary sources as well as interviews with eyewitnesses.

In her opening remarks, White promised "clothes for the whole family of women—daughters as well as mothers and grandmothers—to wear with great comfort, great style and great delight while they discover America." For the Seventh Avenue representatives in the room, she added: "The talent, the inspiration and, above all, the workmanship of our great American designers is unduplicatable anywhere. I think you will agree that the fashions you are about to see possess true native genius."

With that, White introduced the first section: "How did you guess?— red, white and blue." A patriotic parade of models draped in red, white, and blue fashions for day and evening stormed the runway, brandishing hats, umbrellas, and flags made of "Discover America" scarves.[36] It is tempting to speculate that the First Lady herself suggested the red, white, and blue clothes, inspired by her inflight entertainment. Of course, that particular color combination had nothing to do with what was happening in American fashion at the time—or any time, apart from the 1976 Bicentennial celebrations, perhaps—and the committee clearly struggled to find enough red,

white, and blue outfits to fill the runway. Most of the looks included one or two of the colors, rather than all three at once, and this opening section of the show, more than any other, relied on youth-oriented sportswear labels rather than prestigious Seventh Avenue designers: James Galanos, Geoffrey Beene, Rudi Gernreich, and Oscar de la Renta rubbed shoulders with Monte Sano, Mr. Mort, Originala, and Deanna Littell—"this country's answer to England's Mary Quant," as Eugenia Sheppard once described her.[37] (Littell, who designed for the trendsetting Paraphernalia boutique, fit her clothes on her own body and tested them "hanging from a strap in the subway, getting in and out of taxis, walking quickly with big strides. Sooner or later, I found out the kinks.")[38] Marquise and Roxane for Samuel Winston—two labels favored by the First Lady—contributed campaign-ready coat and dress ensembles to this section.

The "Discover America" scarf covered a broad-brimmed hat by Emme, which set off Jenny Chillcott's saucer eyes. "It was about as big as me!" the model remembers. "It wasn't the easiest thing to maneuver on one's head. I said: 'You want me to wear *that?*' But the audience thought it was the best thing since sliced bread."[39] With the hat, she wore a zippered white cotton coat with patch pockets and brass buttons designed by Don Simonelli for Modelia; the same coat had appeared in the February 1 issue of *Vogue*.[40] The scarf also graced the neckline of Kimberly's red knit dress and coat ensemble, modeled by Denise Linden (Helen Hite had worn it for the photo call). Flame-haired Fran Healy wore a red and white printed cotton piqué

Denise Linden in a white Raelson cape over a red Kimberly coat and dress, Jenny Chillcott in a Modelia "shirt coat" of white linen with an Emme hat, and Harriet Simmell in a navy cotton suit with white polka dots by Sarnoff (NARA)

Oscar de la Renta dress and matching coat with navy linen collar and cuffs. While *Women's Wear Daily* had praised the "pretty, pretty" evening gowns in de la Renta's spring collection, his daytime offerings were "really not much more than good little basics in good-looking cottons with a bit of extra trimming"—a description that fits this ensemble perfectly.[41] Though not a standout piece, it was undoubtedly chosen for its patriotic color scheme.

Geoffrey Beene had two outfits in the opening section: a belted red jacket and white skirt and a red cotton piqué midi skirt with navy satin binding and a matching white vest. A Neiman Marcus advertisement that appeared in the March 1 issue of *Vogue* called the midi ensemble "the Goya Gypsy," probably referencing the deep "Goya red" hue Beene had used for Lynda's velvet bridesmaid gowns, inspired by the artist's portrait *Manuel Osorio Manrique de Zuñiga* in the Metropolitan Museum of Art.[42] Nancy White described it as "an enchanting example of the new length for an evening occasion." According to *Women's Wear Daily*, Beene's "unusual summer fabrics . . . might be cotton but have all the couture appeal of wool." However, "any woman who has sweltered through a summer in the city would find it difficult to keep her cool in some of his heavily tailored and heavily weighted cottons. They just seem too rigid for women who enjoy their freedom."[43] Several of the pieces featured in the fashion show survive in museum collections, though their illustrious White House provenance has not been recorded. Beene himself donated the sample to the Metropolitan Museum of Art's Costume Institute.

Luba Marks had started her label, Elite, with her husband, Richard, in 1959. "Her clothes, always young and with it, reach customers at under $100 to around $300," Eugenia Sheppard noted.[44] Her contribution to the White House was a "tiny mess jacket fastened with gold link buttons"

Above left: Pud Gadiot models Geoffrey Beene's red, white, and navy quilted evening midi ensemble on the runway (NARA)

Above: Beene donated the runway sample to the Metropolitan Museum of Art, where he found inspiration for the "Goya" red. (Image copyright © The Metropolitan Museum of Art. Image source: Art Resource, NY)

Left: Pud Gadiot with Sherry Thomas in Nat Kaplan's red, white, and blue pleated gown with culotte skirt and Judy Hinman in Rudi Gernreich (NARA)

paired with "white silk shirt with a Windsor knotted red tie" and "a very short plain dirndl skirt," worn with white tights and flat lace-up shoes. Resembling a school uniform in red, white, and blue, the ensemble was "obviously for the very young," White noted.

Rudi Gernreich's ensemble of linear-patterned red and white linen dhoti (or diaper pants) and a blue and white top was "one of the less conservative" in the show, according to the *New York Times*.[45] This could have come as no surprise to Mrs. Johnson and her guests, who still had the sight of actress Carol Channing in Gernreich's canary-yellow chiffon bloomer dress at Lynda's wedding burned into their retinas.[46] (Before the show, one fashion editor wondered: "Do you think Rudi will show any of his topless things?")[47]

Left: Judy Hinman walks the runway barefoot in Rudi Gernreich's red, white, and blue dhoti ensemble. (Reprinted with permission of the DC Public Library, Star Collection © *Washington Post*)

Right: Rudi Gernreich, wearing Pierre Cardin and seated with Nancy Dickerson and Lynda Robb, watches Judy Hinman model his outfit on the runway. (Getty Images)

The ensemble was undoubtedly chosen by committee member Dorothy LeSueur, who had praised Gernreich's avant-garde, Asian-inspired collection in the *Washington Post* a few weeks earlier.[48] Just as in the designer's spring show, the model, Judy Hinman, "walked out as if she were performing a Thai temple dance, wearing foot-long Fu Manchu fingernails."[49] Hinman's sinuous movements (and bare feet) must have brought back for the First Lady memories of the *fon lep* ("fingernail dance") she'd seen performed in Bangkok in 1966, in which the female dancers wore six-inch-long brass fingernails.[50] From the front row, Gernreich beamed with pride.

A beige, side-buttoned wool coat dress by James Galanos—paired with a bowler-like hat—was one of many similar beige coat dresses from his spring collection. Though the neutral color was intended to be seasonless, *Women's Wear Daily* had complained that "far too many of his clothes were overconstructed and too heavy for a collection billed as spring-summer."[51] Marylin Bender called the designer's overwhelmingly white spring 1968 collection "very much grand ladies in the colonies," adding: "With that perfectionistic Galanos construction, they're the most expensive white outfits going. It would take no less than a $7 cleaner to remove a speck of soot."[52]

While only one-quarter of the clothes in the show were red, white, and blue, virtually all the press images—from the photo call on the White House lawn to the behind-the-scenes newsreel footage—featured these ensembles, even though many of the photos were published in black and white. Some press reports even gave the impression that the entire show consisted of red, white, and blue clothes. But they were just the beginning.

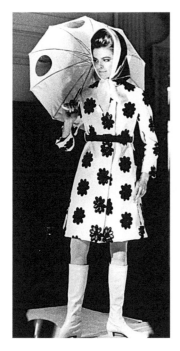

Left: Yolande d'Oultremont models a flowery black and white vinyl raincoat by Bill Blass for Bond Street. (LBJ Library photo by Robert Knudsen)

Center: Mrs. Johnson admired this white linen Adele Simpson ensemble, modeled by Jan Jolley. (LBJ Library photo by Robert Knudsen)

Right: Denise Linden models Teal Traina's striped cotton dress and jacket with a deep "Puritan" collar. (LBJ Library, White House Naval Photographic Unit, Outs Roll 16 of 16 of MP 893, *The President, February 1968*)

The second section, "Travel fashions for the adventure in sight, sound and excitement that will make America the place to be this Summer," presented another side of the "Discover America" theme. This segment was a clear concession to Mrs. Johnson's vision of "good-looking, outdoorsy clothes," though props like tote bags, suitcases, cameras, sunglasses, umbrellas, and binoculars emphasized the theme more than the clothes themselves did.

The first of five Bill Blass ensembles in the show was his black and white vinyl raincoat trimmed with black-eyed Susans, designed for the coat maker Bond Street. The eye-catching coat (today it would be described as "Instagramable") had just appeared in *Vogue* in two colorways; a few weeks later, it would be featured in a fashion spread in the *Saturday Evening Post*, alongside a profile of Blass.[53] The futuristic fabric and oversized floral decoration was reminiscent of similar designs by André Courrèges and Mary Quant, who made a stylized daisy her logo in 1966. Yolande d'Oultremont modeled it, twirling an umbrella with peekaboo plastic panels in front of an image of a Yosemite waterfall.

More black and white ensembles followed. The first of two Adele Simpson outfits in the show was a black "sleeveless coat" paired with a dress of white silk with spotted with black

Left: Jenny Chillcott models a white linen "bathrobe coat" by John Kloss with his black and white jersey dress in "the very important tunic silhouette." (LBJ Library photo by Robert Knudsen)

Right: Gustave Tassell designed his own hats, introducing large brims for spring 1968. (Philadelphia Museum of Art: Gift of the designer, 1973, 1973-33-43)

clown dots. The coat was lined with the same fabric, a tailoring trick duplicated by many of the ensembles in the show. When Simpson's crisp scalloped white linen dress and jacket appeared, Mrs. Johnson was heard to murmur: "Now I like that."[54] (The First Lady had already previewed Simpson's spring collection: "One selection, several maybes.")[55] Teal Traina's black and white striped cotton dress with a white belt and a deep "Puritan collar" was a "great ensemble look for summer," White said.

The next pieces represented "the very important tunic silhouette," as White called it. John Kloss's black V-necked jersey dress bordered with white at the collar and hem—worn under a white linen "bathrobe coat"—was typical of the former architecture student's high-contrast, geometric designs, inspired by abstract art. It was joined by a characteristically minimalist Gustave Tassell tunic and skirt combination in two colorways: heavy black silk over white and white linen over black. Both were shown with flat, broad-brimmed black straw hats. "Tassell always designs the hats for his clothes," Bernadine Morris explained. "This time, they have big brims."[56]

Another Blass look, a cream windowpane-check wool coat lined in brown silk, was belted with metal links at one side. In her remarks, Nancy White declared it "a handsome way to visit a new town." The *New York Times* reported that "there was wild applause" when the model removed the coat on the runway to reveal a brown silk dress with matching metal fastenings.[57]

A gray Adolphe Zelinka vest and pleated skirt paired with a pussycat bow blouse with brown polka dots may have

Left: This window-pane-check wool coat by Bill Blass, belted with metal links at the side, was responsible for a dramatic reveal on the runway. (From the collection of the Goldstein Museum of Design, Gift of Sylvia Druy)

Right: Model Judy Dennis removed the coat to reveal the brown silk lining and matching dress, with hardware identical to that of the coat. (From the collection of the Goldstein Museum of Design, Gift of Sylvia Druy)

Below: Office-ready junior ensembles by Adolphe Zelinka, Rembrandt, and Harvey Berin (LBJ Library photo by Robert Knudsen)

looked like office attire, but the short hemline indicated that it was actually from the juniors' department. The vest of "noncrushable linen"—meaning rayon—was lined in the same fabric as the blouse. From junior label Sportwhirl, there was a blue gingham dress "that resembled a milkmaid costume," according to one reporter.[58] By the late '6os, many designers and department stores were exploring so-called boutique lines, trendy and inexpensive clothes aimed at the growing teen market. The practice started in Paris, with Yves Saint Laurent's Rive Gauche ready-to-wear line, an accessible (if not exactly inexpensive) alternative to couture. But the concept was inspired by actual boutiques patronized by young people with more dash than cash, like those found on the King's Road in London, or Paraphernalia, the modernist design collective with go-go girls dancing in the windows, which opened in New York in 1965. Not just teenagers but secretaries and young socialites—including Mrs. Kennedy—shopped the boutiques, attracted by low prices, loud rock music, and hip salesgirls sporting clothes by unknown designers like Betsey Johnson.[59] For these women, the epicenter of the fashion world no longer meant Paris but Greenwich Village or London's Chelsea neighborhood. Department stores took note and began opening their own in-house boutiques to attract a youthful clientele.

The first of three Mollie Parnis creations to appear on the runway was what White called "one of the most ingenious costumes of the season: a tiny flowered vest and a short skirt zippered over a shirtwaist dress of green silk. Put the parts together as you will." The model, Peggy Parke, removed the vest and stepped out of the skirt on the runway to reveal the dress, which was even shorter.[60] Offering several possible outfits in one, the ensemble (along with other three-in-one costumes Parnis produced) helps explain the designer's appeal to the cost-conscious First Lady.

Two vibrant patterned dresses by Anne Fogarty shared the runway, one in an abstract print, the other in navy and white plaid. "All wash and wear, almost in a matter of minutes," White assured the audience. Fogarty, who had started her fashion career as a model for Hattie Carnegie, was known for her youthful, romantic approach to fashion, though it had been a long time since she had won her 1951 Coty Award. Then it was Blass's turn again; Judy Dennis modeled his thigh-skimming coat of hot orange silk with yellow and purple flowers over a puckered yellow silk dress of the same length that matched the coat's lining.

B. H. Wragge's entry, a mint-green and pink plaid ensemble, really did discover America in style. In May 1968, the sleeveless silk kaftan and matching culottes were featured alongside other rainbow-hued Wragge fashions in an eight-page *Vogue* color advertising supplement for Kodak Instamatic cameras, shot on a transatlantic trip aboard the SS *United States*. Lynda Robb was a longtime fan of the high-end sportswear label; its designer, Adrienne "Adri" Steckling, was almost as tall as Lynda and designed with her own needs mind. She was known for her culotte ensembles, which she promoted as an alternative to pants. "They gave me the convenience of pants but the feeling of a skirt," she explained. "It turned out that appealed to other women too. I just didn't decide 'Let there be culottes.'"[61]

A pair of pink satin evening pajamas by Bill Blass—one of the few trouser ensembles in the show—opened the third section, which the program
dubbed "Festival Fashions—for enjoying the ever growing wealth of the
visual and performing arts in our country." Pajamas first left the house in
the 1930s, when women wore fashionable, wide-legged versions to the
beach, parties, and informal dinners; some daring young things even wore
them to the theater. Reintroduced in Italy in the mid-1960s as eveningwear,
pajamas represented "a splurge of Eastern fantaisie, optical illusion, brash
invention—on an over-your-traces kick, dusk to dawn," *Vogue* gushed in
1965. Indeed, pajamas seemed to have encouraged women to indulge in
adventurous sartorial role-playing. Exotic textiles and accessories like os-
trich feathers, chandelier earrings, and turbans reflected the style's Eastern
origins. Blass's version had a Japanese-inspired print and jeweled epaulettes
and cuffs—rare in his oeuvre. Elaborate bouffant hairdos further refuted
any notion that the wearer had just rolled out of bed. Evening pajamas
were a "heavenly way to dress for small dinners, parties, dancing in the
moonlight," *Vogue* suggested.[62] Far from sleepwear, these ensembles were
made for staying up all night.

A group of fashions in the romantic, neo-Victorian mode were simultaneously youthful and nostalgic; their girlish ruffles, gingham, and polka dots
were balanced by thigh-high hemlines. (In April, Bill Cunningham would
dub this trend "Little-Miss-Muffet femininity.")[63] Adolfo contributed a
formal midi skirt covered in three-dimensional silk daisies, paired with a
sleeveless black jersey blouse; true to his roots as a milliner, he created a
matching flower-trimmed hat, which the model, Judy Dennis, carried.[64]

Above left: Judy Dennis models Adolfo's evening midi covered ın three-dımen-sional silk daisies, a matching hat in her hand. (LBJ Library, White House Naval Photographic Unit, Outs Roll 16 of 16 of MP 893, *The President, February 1968*)

Above right: Youthful, nostalgic styles by Travilla (*left and center*) and Junior Sophisticates (LBJ Library photo by Robert Knudsen)

Right: Pauline Trigère's "romantic" strapless white organdy midi dress with a sheer cropped blouse caught the First Lady's eye. (Photo courtesy of the Kent State University Museum)

Left: Chester Weinberg's midi dress is strewn with three-dimensional silk forget-me-nots; on the runway, the green sash was tied in front. (From the collection of the Goldstein Museum of Design, Gift of Ann Ferris)

Right: Fluttering flowers also sprouted from Weinberg's net coat, worn over a strapless gown. (LBJ Library, White House Naval Photographic Unit, Outs Roll 16 of 16 of MP 893, *The President, February 1968*)

(Some of his hats also appeared in the show.) A strapless white organdy midi dress with a lacy cropped blouse by Pauline Trigère caught the First Lady's eye. "That's a romantic dress," she said with enthusiasm.[65] Abell later sent her a photo of the dress with an attached note reading: "I could pursue the possibility of having floor length or day time." But Mrs. Johnson apparently had a change of heart, responding: "Never mind." The runway sample—a size 0—survives today in the Kent State University Museum. In 1982, manufacturer Jerry Silverman and designer Shannon Rodgers— business partners and life partners who participated in the show—donated their personal costume collection to the museum, subsequently enlisting their friend Trigère and many other fashion industry colleagues to donate garments, sketchbooks, and archival materials.[66]

It was traditional for fashion shows to end with evening gowns—or, as the program described them, "gala dresses dedicated to the American Beauty in every woman" for "star spangled evenings." The *New York Post* described the show's evening looks as "romantic and feminine" with "shapely waistlines and skirts that made a point of not sweeping the floor."[67] Here, however, the show abandoned all pretense of a travel theme. "Who could think of packing yards of white organdy into a suitcase?" the *Washington Post*

Helen Hite models Geoffrey Beene's organdy blouse and gingham maxi skirt embroidered with straw flowers and trimmed with green velvet ribbon. (LBJ Library photo by Robert Knudsen)

asked.[68] It would certainly crush the three-dimensional silk forget-me-nots that decorated a tulle and organza Chester Weinberg midi that White called "a dress that celebrates girlishness . . . sashed with the biggest green taffeta bow of all time." Another Weinberg dress, this one entirely white with a long skirt and a satin sash, was similarly blooming with three-dimensional flowers. As *Women's Wear Daily* said of his spring 1968 collection, "Chester Weinberg certainly understands the meaning of romance."[69]

Geoffrey Beene's spring collection "was a blend of Monet and Toulouse Lautrec magic," according to the *Chicago Tribune*. Riding high on his newfound fame as Lynda Bird's wedding dress designer, Beene doubled his prices and let loose his fantasies, showing clothes that bordered on costume. The organdy blouse and straw-embroidered gingham maxi skirt trimmed with green velvet ribbon that appeared on the White House runway were originally shown on a model wearing a lacquered straw boater, evoking the full-length summer day dresses of the *fin-de-siècle*, as painted by Renoir and Manet.[70] "Gingham turns sophisticated," the *New York Times* declared of the old-fashioned, feminine fabric that also resurfaced in Chester Weinberg's, George Halley's, and Adolfo's collections.[71]

Oscar de la Renta's white organza "portrait dress," paired with a ruffled stole, also sprouted fluttering floral trimmings. Renée Hunter modeled

a much different de la Renta gown, of vibrant silk striped organza with a black ribbon winding around the empire waist and over one shoulder. Gayle Kirkpatrick—the male designer behind the Atelier label—had a flair for edgy but affordable sportswear. He contributed a white linen shirtdress with a crimson velvet sash, one of many evening shirtdresses in the spring collections. A gown of pleated yellow-rose-of-Texas chiffon by Hannah Troy seemed calculated to appeal to the First Lady, as did a beaded white Mollie Parnis gown trimmed with pale yellow velvet ribbon.

Sarmi's green chiffon gown was a tried-and-true silhouette he'd used in several collections, combining a full skirt with bow at the waist and a heavily embellished bodice or jacket with short sleeves and a crew neck.[72] "Both the Sarmi and Mollie Parnis fashions are designed primarily for the adult, solid gold socialite," the *Philadelphia Inquirer* had noted approvingly in its review of their spring collections. "The designers know exactly what they're doing and they don't give a hoot about keeping up with the kiddies."[73] The pressure designers faced to choose between pleasing the traditional "adult" fashion audience and enticing the emerging demographic of "kiddies" was a pervasive theme of American fashion journalism in 1968. By presenting a cross-section of diverse designers, the White House fashion show inadvertently highlighted these tensions.

George Halley's strapless, seafoam-green gown with a jeweled bodice had a matching jeweled jacket, which the model, Claudia Halley look-alike Harriet Simmell, removed on the runway. Like most of Halley's eveningwear, it is a romantic, feminine, expensive-looking garment that barely touches the body, chiffon flowing from an Empire waistline into a full skirt made for dancing. Combining sixties chic with Old Hollywood glamour, it captures the seductively original viewpoint of the designer *Women's Wear Daily* described as being "in a lovely world of his own."[74]

Left: Renée Hunter models Oscar de la Renta's striped silk organza gown trimmed with a black ribbon. (LBJ Library, White House Naval Photographic Unit, Outs Roll 16 of 16 of MP 893, *The President, February 1968*)

Right: Pat Mori models Hannah Troy's pleated yellow-rose-of-Texas chiffon gown. (LBJ Library photo by Robert Knudsen)

Left: Harriet Simmell models George Halley's strapless seafoam-green chiffon gown with a jeweled bodice and jacket. (LBJ Library photo by Robert Knudsen)

Right: Roxane's cotton lace gown for Samuel Winston—modeled by Mozella Roberts—was the clear favorite among the governors' wives. (Philadelphia Museum of Art: Anonymous gift from the family of Mrs. Charlotte Dorrance Wright, 1978, 1978-72-35a,b)

But at least one reporter who covered his spring show had suggested that Halley's high-waisted silhouettes made his models look pregnant.[75]

The final parade of white gowns was silhouetted against a slide showing the marble columns of the White House itself. The clear crowd favorite was a floor-length cotton lace shirtdress by one of Mrs. Johnson's regular designers, Roxane Kaminstein for Samuel Winston, modeled by Mozella Roberts; an example, now missing its belt, survives in the Philadelphia Museum of Art.[76] Nancy White hailed it as "sheer femininity from top to toe." A second Roxane gown on the runway had been singled out in the *Philadelphia Enquirer*'s Press Week coverage as "her special stunt . . . a white organdie shirt dress, plaided all over in blocks of tiny sequins."[77] Winston had hired Roxane and Charles James to design his clothes in the 1950s; the mercurial James soon left the company, accusing Roxane of stealing his ideas. But she claimed to draw her inspiration from her previous career as a fashion buyer, which had familiarized her with women's tastes and needs. A 1960 press release celebrating her Coty Award—which was still being reprinted verbatim in ads and newspaper articles years later—touted Roxane's "seemingly infallible sense of wearability, no matter how advanced the silhouette or how luxurious the effect."[78]

Galanos "goes all out for tailored evening clothes," according to the *New York Times*.[79] The show featured his white silk gazar gown with dramatic leg-o'-mutton sleeves and an equally eye-catching jeweled bib of emerald green and crystalline beading. A satin version of the on-trend ribbed wool evening shirtdress with white lizard belt shown on the runway is preserved

in the Kent State University Museum. Curiously, *Women's Wear Daily* had been disappointed by the eveningwear in his spring collection; admittedly, though, the reporter was exhausted from sitting through a three-hour presentation of 179 looks.[80]

The show saved two of the First Lady's eveningwear go-tos, George Stavropoulos and John Moore, for last. Stavropoulos contributed a white crepe "goddess gown" with a toga-like drape that left one arm bare and the other swathed by a floating bias panel. Moore's bias-cut sleeveless crepe gown looked simple from the front but had an elegantly draped back. Instead of the traditional white-gowned bride, a red, white, and blue strapless chiffon number by Sarmi—pin-pleated and trimmed with the designer's signature bow—brought the show to a rousingly patriotic conclusion; it was one of several "tri-color chiffons in wide bands [of] color" in his spring collection.[81] The other models joined the gowned goddesses onstage, and Mrs. Johnson shook their hands before making her way backstage to congratulate the rest of the team.[82]

As well as providing summer travel inspiration, the *New York Post* observed that "for a governor's lady, in an election year, the show was surely a shopping blessing, now that campaigning has become such a high exposure family affair."[83] However, the reporters in the room could not help noticing the disconnect between the cutting-edge fashions on display and

Instead of a wedding dress, Denise Linden closed the show in a red, white, and blue strapless chiffon gown by Sarmi. (LBJ Library photo by Robert Knudsen)

The final tableau of white evening gowns—and one in red, white, and blue—by (from left) Oscar de la Renta, Roxane for Samuel Winston, Mollie Parnis, Malcolm Starr, John Moore, Sarmi, George Stavroupoulos, James Galanos, Galanos, Parnis, and Chester Weinberg (LBJ Library photo by Robert Knudsen)

the more conservative clothes worn by the political wives. "There were miniskirts on the runway aplenty and colored stockings, too. But not in the audience. The governors' ladies ran to skirts just at or a bit below the knee and 'stocking-colored' hosiery." [84]

Not all the runway looks were hits with this group. While "there was nothing on view to traumatize," the comments heard from most of the guests were "That would be perfect for my daughter" or "Who over 40 wears a size eight?"[85] They "were noticeably cool to those miniskirts displayed."[86] Margery Clifford, whose husband was LBJ's secretary of defense, admitted: "I think the minis are such fun. I can't wear them, but then I've never been fascinated by my knees."[87] (She preferred John Moore's white crepe gown with the "beautiful back.") Meredith Docking, wife of the Kansas governor, "thought it was a beautiful show but doubted the clothes were 'wearable.'"[88] Even Lynda Robb said she wasn't likely to buy any of the runway looks—"not on a Captain's pay." Her husband, Chuck, was due to depart for Vietnam in May.[89]

The guests "saved their biggest applause for long evening gowns emphasizing the feminine look."[90] Happy Rockefeller—representing New York, the home of the garment industry—told reporters that "there were many perfectly heavenly things and it was in excellent taste."[91] Asked if she'd seen anything in the show suitable for campaigning, she deflected the pointed reference to her husband's expected presidential run, answering: "No, but I saw a lot of clothes I'd like to wear."[92] She confessed that she had already ordered herself a midi skirt for the fall.[93] "A woman in her 40s should think twice before wearing a miniskirt," she added, self-deprecatingly."[94] Betty Williams announced she was "going to go home and lose 20 pounds instead of the 10 I originally planned on"; Vera Williams, the wife of the Arizona governor, delivered a brutal backhanded compliment when she remarked of the new midi length: "That's for me—I'm naturally dowdy."[95]

As for the jaded fashion industry professionals in the crowd, they realized that they were making history that day. "I've forgotten many fashion shows I have attended," Barbara Cloud, the longtime fashion editor of the *Pittsburgh-Post Gazette* wrote decades later. "But not this one."[96] Jeanne Campbell saved her program, place cards, menu, and other mementos, and she was not the only designer to do so. Jerry Silverman's invitation is preserved in his archive.[97] Gernreich kept his place card, invitation, menu, security pass, and program—signed by his tablemates, including Nina Hyde, China Machado, Nancy Dickerson, and Lynda Robb, who wrote a "J" before remembering that she had a new last name. The designer called his visit to the White House a "tremendous thrill"—a sentiment

Rudi Gernreich's tablemates signed his program, which he initialed "R.G." (Courtesy of the FIDM Museum at the Fashion Institute of Design & Merchandising, Los Angeles, CA, Rudi Gernreich Archive, Bequest of the Rudi Gernreich Estate)

many of his colleagues echoed.[98] Designer Don Simonelli was starstruck, remarking, "Imagine, sitting in the White House watching my clothes on a runway."[99] George Stavropoulos told the *Washington Post:* "It is a great honor for me."[100] In his thank-you note to Mrs. Johnson, Chester Weinberg summed up the feelings of many of the participants: "I am still trembling from the excitement of lunching at the White House with you & your many distinguished guests. For me this was a great moment in my life, for Fashion this was a great moment, truly an important one. You have given American Designers a new dignity."[101]

Nancy White called the event nothing less than "one of the greatest things that ever happened to American fashion."[102] While *Harper's Bazaar* did not actually cover the fashion show—as a monthly publication with a long lead time, it likely could not do so in a timely manner—it is clear that the content of the show influenced the magazine's editorial layouts for months afterward. All three Galanos pieces from the runway showed up in a May 1968 spread. The caption to the "grand shirt dinner dress" photo read: "The impression of good looks, health and a glorious American penchant for ease, in a single joyous fashion statement. . . . Its only ornament: the woman who wears it." The silk gazar gown with the jeweled bib had also appeared in a Bonwit Teller ad in the April issue, sketched by Kenneth Paul Block.[103] The same issue featured a large ad for Sheffield watches, the show's sponsor.

An Anne Fogarty ad in the June 1968 issue showed a long-sleeved version of the brown, navy, and white printed dress from the runway; a ruffled white cotton shirtdress by Fogarty, which had been cut from the show at the last minute, was also featured in an editorial layout that month. The "supremely seductive" George Stavropoulos and John Moore goddess gowns from the finale appeared together in a March article titled "The Olympian Game," paired with Kenneth Jay Lane earrings. And in February, an eight-page spread incongruously paired Broadway actors like Joel Grey and Jerry Orbach with models in spring knitwear and brightly colored, broad-brimmed hats by Emme, identical to the style customized with the "Discover America" scarf for White House the runway.[104]

Newspapers across the country picked up Associated Press correspondent Frances Lewine's story on the show, along with a photo of models waving flags made of "Discover America" scarves on the runway, the State Dining Room's distinctive McKim, Mead, and White chandelier in the foreground. (Competing wire service United Press International released a more fashion-forward photo, showing Rudi Gernreich watching his daring ensemble on the runway; once again, however, the chandelier figured prominently, as did George Healy's pensive portrait of Abraham Lincoln over the mantlepiece.) "History's first White House fashion show had it all,"

Lewine wrote. "Fancy clothes, beautiful models and a gilded setting—and the President of the United States." She added, "Everyone in the garment industry—the nation's fourth largest—was grateful" to Mrs. Johnson for the invitation to the White House.[105]

The First Lady, in turn, sent handwritten thank-you notes to everyone involved in the show: the models, the behind-the-scenes helpers, and the organizing committee. Eleanor Lambert found a bouquet from Mrs. Johnson waiting for her in her room at the Madison Hotel.[106] To Eleni Epstein, the First Lady wrote: "Now that the runway has disappeared from the Dining Room, the models have gone, and the last bobby pin has been swept up from the Blue Room, it hardly seems possible that last week we had an exciting fashion show here at the White House."[107]

7

The Politics of Fashion

"Nobody knows why exactly a fashion show has never been held at the White House before," the *Pittsburgh Press* noted at the time.[1] Even more perplexing are the reasons it never happened again. Certainly, those who witnessed it—and organized it—expected that its success would pave the way for many similar events in the future.[2] "Now that it has happened once, it hardly seems likely that the first fashion show in the White House will be the last," Eugenia Sheppard declared. "America's First Ladies have become steadily more fashion conscious over the last 15 years, and the public, far from objecting, shows every sign of liking them that way.... After this, there's no reason why both designers and women shouldn't look forward to a semi-annual show of American fashions in the best possible American setting."[3]

But the Leap Day event proved to be a once-in-a-lifetime happening. For all their careful planning and good intentions, Mrs. Johnson and her staff did not anticipate the myriad dangers of mixing fashion and politics. As soon as the show was formally announced, on February 21, telegrams poured in from people across the country, lobbying for roles in the event. Marjorie Carne, the executive director of California Fashion Creators, urged the organizers to include California designers as well as Seventh Avenue stalwarts. Boston's Carol Nashe Model Agency offered to donate the services (and travel expenses) of a "beautiful five foot seven size 8–10 negress professional fashion model," pointing out: "Boston is the birth place of our great nation."[4]

In the aftermath of the show, another flurry of telegrams arrived. Designers from DC to Dallas complained that they had been left out. The president of the Philadelphia Convention and Tourist Bureau protested that there were not enough images of his city in the slide show. And, though it had taken Dickerson, Abell, Lambert, and assorted fashion industry representatives years to convince Mrs. Johnson to host a fashion show, it finally happened at the worst possible time, midway through the Tet Offensive, the uprising that took its name from Vietnam's Lunar New Year celebrations. On February 18, just days before the show, the Pentagon had announced the Vietnam War's highest weekly death toll: 543 American soldiers lost. An angrily scrawled letter to Mrs. Johnson preserved in the Johnson Presidential Library reads: "Have you given up Highway beautification for Fashion Shows? How much longer do you all in The White House expect to insult our HARD Core Service men, Both in Vietnam and those poor suckers imprisoned in Korea? You all can fly while they Die and suffer. What a disgrace."[5]

Sharon Francis remembered the event and its red, white, and blue color scheme as a tribute to the war effort rather than an insensitive snub. "We all were constantly aware of the increasing toll being taken by the Vietnam War on American lives and enjoyments," she said.[6] However, the gesture backfired, and the fashion show ended up being another black mark against the Johnson administration. On the same day that the show took place, the Kerner Commission issued its report on the racial unrest of the previous summer, blaming "white racism" for the violence. For New York senator Robert F. Kennedy, LBJ's dismissive response to the report was further evidence "that this country is on a perilous course"; on March 16, he announced his candidacy for the Democratic presidential nomination, running against the incumbent. Two weeks later, on March 31, President Johnson shocked the country by announcing that he would not seek reelection. (Perhaps he was also stung by campaign buttons advocating "ABJ"—"Anyone But Johnson.") Kennedy was assassinated in Los Angeles on June 6; Republican Richard Nixon (who had been Eisenhower's vice president) would win a narrow victory over Vice President Hubert Humphrey that November. The *Pittsburgh Press* described "brightly clad young Nixon Girls" lining up the city's Civic Arena to greet Nixon as he arrived at a campaign rally just days before the election, wearing paper dresses emblazoned with his name in red, white, and blue. These disposable dresses enjoyed a brief vogue in the turbulent 1960s, when young people literally wore their politics on their sleeves—but were prepared to discard them like so much used Kleenex.

Waste Basket Boutique by Mars of Asheville, North Carolina, produced a Nixon campaign dress of screen-printed paper. (Artokoloro/Alamy Stock Photo)

Paper dresses printed with photos of 1968 presidential candidates, from left, Hubert Humphrey, Eugene McCarthy, Nelson Rockefeller, Ronald Reagan and Richard Nixon (Oregon Historical Society/ George Moore Collection)

Although there was no way of knowing it on February 29, 1968 would be remembered as a year of revolution.[7] Even as the models walked the runway, labor organizer Cesar Chavez was midway through a 25-day fast protesting violence against striking migrant farmworkers. Martin Luther King Jr. was assassinated on April 4. Arthur Ashe became the first Black man to win a Grand Slam tournament; Shirley Chisholm became the first Black woman elected to Congress. The year 1968 brought the Prague Spring, the Civil Rights Act, and the American Indian Movement. In Mexico City, two American Olympic medalists, Tommie Smith and John Carlos, raised their fists in Black Power salutes on the podium. At the Miss America pageant in Atlantic City, protestors threw their bras (along with makeup, girdles, high heels, and issues of *Playboy* and *Cosmopolitan*) into a trash can. The Democratic National Convention was marred by violence as demonstrators chanted, "The whole world is watching."

All of these social and political upheavals—amplified and magnified by mass media—affected the fashion industry. As historian Betty Luther Hillman has pointed out, "knowing that the eyes of the world were upon them helps to explain why some activists used dress and hairstyles as visual cues to signify their political goals."[8] In turn, these protest styles challenged—and sometimes inspired—mainstream fashions. On April 15, in a front-page article headlined "Political, Social Factors Enter Fall Dress Picture," *Women's Wear Daily* predicted a disappointing fall season for worried American designers and manufacturers, following "uneven" spring and summer sales. "Developments on the political, social and economic horizons will affect their business more profoundly than perhaps in past seasons, and weigh more heavily than questions of styling, colors and prices." Factors cited included the unpredictable course of the Vietnam War, "possible new racial disturbances this summer, which would affect retail sales," the rising costs of fabrics and wages, and the fluctuating stock market. "The still unanswered question of skirt lengths in the minds of many consumers is another factor cited by manufacturers, many of whom have settled this matter." Malcolm Starr, who was enjoying a 15 percent boost in sales in the wake of his visit to the White House, told *Women's Wear Daily:* "If we have a Vietnam peace settlement, then business should be good. . . . However, if we have a lot of racial unrest in New York and other large cities across the country, it can seriously affect our shipping." Nat Rubin of Rembrandt, another label represented in the show, said the spring season had been "a roller coaster ride."[9]

At a time of rapid fluctuations in American manners and mores, fashion was a visible barometer of social change. As Hillman has pointed out, "broader shifts in women's lives were often discussed alongside media conversations about pants and miniskirts."[10] Equal rights manifested itself in unisex dressing. Women adopted pants and rejected sartorial markers of middle-class femininity like bras, girdles, and makeup. Men wore their hair long, pushing back against the crew cuts associated with "LBJ's War." Civil rights activists expressed their resistance to Caucasian cultural norms by wearing exaggerated Afros and traditional African clothing (or, alternatively, military-inspired garb). Savvy politicians took note of fashion's cultural cachet and statement-making power. "In the 1960's, fashion spilled out of the closet and into politics, the arts and big business," Marylin Bender of the *New York Times* reflected in 1969. "Politician's wives and social climbers learned to drop designer names. The proper answer to the formerly impertinent question, 'Whose dress are you wearing?' was not, as Lady Bird Johnson, Mary Lindsay [the down-to-earth wife of New York's mayor] and Happy Rockefeller discovered, 'My own.'"[11]

The feminine, romantic look so prevalent and so well received on the White House runway was dead by the fall. "Though the white organdies and the bows and ruffles looked charming by themselves, or even in twos and threes, when they come in droves they look as saccharine as a sugar bowl," Eugenia Sheppard declared. "With its passion for playing follow-the-leader, 7th Ave. really finished the ruffle along with the whole ingénue bit for a while."[12] Indeed, it looked as if fashion itself was finished—fashion as Mrs. Johnson and her generation knew it, at least. The White House fashion show was the swansong of an industry that, unbeknownst to itself, was already obsolete. American fashion—indeed, the very meaning of fashion—was in the midst of a violent metamorphosis. Formality, luxury, homogeneity, seasonality—all of fashion's traditional hallmarks were swiftly losing their cultural capital. "There's no one way to look any more," Bill Blass said. "The best way to look is free."[13]

In the late 1960s, the disaffected youth of the Left Bank (Rive Gauche) neighborhood of Paris trawled the city's open-air flea markets looking for romantic embellishments like fringed shawls, Indian jewelry, and antique lace. French designers began to "take this costumey rich mood and raise it up to couture" but risked having their clothes dubbed "hippy" in the process—a term that simultaneously suggested intellectual, moral, and material poverty. "No doubt the lesser houses will be sewing on all the lace and feathers and fringe which the suppliers are reportedly supplying by the bagful," *Women's Wear Daily* sniffed in January 1968, as Parisian couturiers prepared their spring collections. "The better houses, let's hope, will let their new, free, underground spirit lead them . . . to the essence of the whole bit: Beautiful Individualism. . . . What, after all, are the hippies creating with their extravagance but a pauper's notion of Luxury?"[14]

What the American media failed to recognize was that a similar phenomenon was already taking place right under their noses. In 1967, young people had flocked to San Francisco for the so-called Summer of Love, where customized clothing became a canvas for personal and political ideologies. Young people began looking beyond the boutiques, buying their clothes in secondhand shops and army surplus stores.[15] The Peace Corps—established by President Kennedy in 1961—encouraged a generation of young Americans to travel the globe, bringing back a passion for ethnic handcrafts. The nascent environmental movement sparked a backlash against leather, fur, and mass production. And it wasn't just the younger generation that was swayed by the counterculture. Thanks to the war, inflation, and the never-ending hemline debate, consumer confidence in fashion magazines—and the fashion industry in general—was replaced by a rebellious cynicism.

The role of the First Lady as a fashion influencer was also in flux. In 1960, the appearance of a young, fashion-forward potential First Lady on the political scene had prompted much soul-searching among the fashion press. As the *New York Times* mused two months before Election Day:

When Jacqueline Kennedy, then five days the wife of a Presidential nominee, stepped aboard the family yacht in Hyannis Port, Mass., wearing an orange pullover sweater, shocking pink Capri pants and a *bouffant* hairdo that gamboled merrily in the breeze, even those newsmen present who could not tell shocking pink from Windsor Rose knew they were witnessing something of possibly vast political consequences.

Political pollsters may not know exactly what The Women's Vote is, but they know it exists. They know it can be swayed by such imponderables as Tom Dewey's mustache. What, then, is to keep it from being influenced by a pair of pink Capri pants?

This traumatizing possibility gives new urgency to a hard, and largely unrecorded fact of political life: namely, that Presidents' wives—and, for that matter, would-be Presidents' wives—are faced by such a Delicate Dilemma as Presidents never dream of. While the average woman need dress only to please herself or her husband or her bridge club, the President's wife must dress to please everybody. This, of course, is impossible. And any First Lady who could do it could probably handle Congress with one hand lashed behind her back and would clearly deserve to be President.

Casual sexism notwithstanding, the *Times* was on to something. Kennedy's "devil-may-care chic" was "as troublesome to some women as Mrs. Nixon's conservative perfection." It also emphasized her youth, which, like her fashionable wardrobe, was both a political asset and a political liability.

Disaster lurks near every Senate wives' tea. If the First Lady showed up hatless, she would have the good folk of the millinery industry camping on the White House lawn; if she refused to wear fur, the lobbying of the fur trappers' associations would put the oil and railroad chaps to shame; if she expressed a distaste for Oriental pearls she might involve us in an international incident; and if she were to commit the gross blunder of arguing the superiority of Paris couture, the whole of Seventh Avenue would set up a how to drown out the tortured cacophony of a defense budget hearing. They might restrain themselves from hanging her in effigy in the garment center, but what, next election time, would they do to her husband? One begins to see the gravity of her situation.

Although the *Times* was exaggerating for comic effect, similar issues had dogged the wives of kings, emperors, and heads of state for generations. And Kennedy—after temporarily popularizing the pillbox—was, indeed, blamed for the decline of hats later in her tenure, as was her husband, who disliked wearing them.

The *Times* recognized that the First Lady was in an impossible situation. "If she is overly chic, she may lose the common touch (the only other woman who so clearly confronts this danger is the television saleslady, who would drive soap detergent manufacturers to the wall if she delivered her pitch while clad in Dior's latest departure)." However, if her clothes were too drab, "many will complain that she is not Fulfilling her Duty as a Representative of the American Way of Life." Like the soap saleslady, the First Lady had something to sell: American womanhood, and specifically American fashion. And the fashion press—"which opens a First Lady's closet doors to the public"—could not only influence votes but decide the fate of America's fourth largest industry.[16]

The White House fashion show had a lasting impact on its participants as well as the Johnson administration. The storm that had canceled so many flights out of New York that morning hit the capital in the afternoon. "We came out of the White House and there's a blizzard going on!" Lynda Hatch remembered. "The girls who flew out that day said it was the worst flight—they really thought they were done for." Hatch caught a train home to New Jersey instead.[17] Sherry Thomas and Peggy Parke took the train back to the city together; Thomas got engaged to her Vietnam-vet boyfriend that same night. Fran Healy stayed in Washington with her sister.

All the models "recognized that this show was something special that they would probably tell their children and grandchildren about," Barbara Cloud noted.[18] Denise Linden took home three "Discover America" scarf flags as souvenirs for her children.[19] "Just think of history books and all that has taken place in the White House," she said. "And there I am having fittings in Lincoln's bedroom." Thomas, too, took, home a scarf, but the Mannequin agency made all the models give them back—something Thomas deeply regrets today. (She framed the White House matchbook she'd swiped as a souvenir and hung it on her wall.) Bonnie Pfeifer didn't take any trophies, but she was so enamored with the chain belt of the Ellen Brooke ensemble she modeled on the runway that she says: "I wore, like, 800 chain belts for two years after that!"[20] Many of the models exchanged autographs in their programs and saved them as keepsakes.[21]

Though the models of 1968, in general, enjoyed longer careers than their modern-day counterparts, most retired or moved on to new jobs within a few years of their visit to the White House. Thomas had a three-decade career in law enforcement, during which she rarely talked about her modeling days. "The one thing nobody in the police world wants to hear about is that you were a model," she laughs.[22] Thomas kept in touch with Helen Hite, the Lynda look-alike, who had an equally surprising second act: by 1973, she was bodyguard to Princess Muna, the ex-wife of King Hussein of Jordan, who was living in the Watergate Hotel. The "glamorous six-foot-tall American model . . . is said to have a considerable knowledge of the use of firearms," syndicated gossip columnist Igor Cassini (Oleg's brother) reported, adding a full three inches to Hite's height. "She claims to be directly answerable to King Hussein himself for his ex-wife's safety."[23]

Pat Mori parlayed her fashion industry experience and connections into opening a boutique, Pat's Petunia, on the Upper East Side, where she sold art objects including paintings by former model Yvonne Presser and padded picture frames by interior designer Helene Batoff.[24] Lynda Hatch, too, opened a shop, after raising a family; she enrolled in college at the age of 40 and now edits medical texts.[25] Renée Hunter went on to work as a fashion director at Bloomingdale's and a buyer at Saks Fifth Avenue; Pud Gadiot became designer Hanae Mori's New York boutique manager.[26] Judy Hinman designed jewelry that was sold at Henri Bendel; "I started making one-of-a-kind things at home for friends and it snowballed," she told the *Daily News.*[27] She remarried, then opened her own New York modeling agency, Foster-Fell Model Management, with her husband.[28] Jenny Chillcott Garrigues opened an interior design business in Palm Beach, which she still runs today. Toni Bailey worked in public relations for Le Champs, a shopping center in the Watergate complex, but died of leukemia at the age of 47.[29] Bonnie Pfeifer parlayed her appearance on the White House runway into a successful print modeling career, working with Ralph Lauren and Calvin Klein; today, she is focused on philanthropy and real estate.[30]

Meanwhile, the designers and industry insiders dined out on their brush with history, both literally and figuratively. Within weeks of the show, Dorothy LeSueur and Adele Simpson were invited back to the White House as dinner guests. LeSueur sat at the First Lady's table for the State Dinner in honor of President José Trejos of Costa Rica. Mrs. Johnson invited Simpson and her husband to dinner with Imelda Marcos, who was visiting the United States for medical treatment, "because I like them and because Mrs. Marcos likes fashion."[31] In 1971, Mollie Parnis took a page from Mrs. Johnson's beautification book and launched the "Dress Up Your Neighborhood" initiative to encourage improvements to New York's inner city; in 1975, she founded a similar project in Israel.[32]

If Eleanor Lambert felt constrained by working with the White House, she got to do things her way five years later when she organized the Versailles '73 fashion show—an equally patriotic but far more glamorous affair, pitting five top American designers against their Parisian counterparts in another landmark venue, the Royal Theater at the Palace of Versailles.[33] The project reunited Lambert with Bill Blass, Oscar de la Renta, China

Machado, and Fran Healy, Oscar's house model. In many ways, the 1968 White House fashion show can be viewed as a warm-up to Versailles '73, though the latter's far superior production values and focus on a handful of high-end designers implies lessons learned. Lambert was 70 years old at the time; America's so-called Empress of Fashion would live to be 100, dying in 2003.

At the 1969 inaugural ball held at the Smithsonian Institution, President Nixon said of his wife's Harvey Berin gown, "I like all of Pat's dresses, particularly this one tonight, and ... when she gets finished with it, you'll get it at the Smithsonian." (Richard Nixon Presidential Library and Museum photo by Oliver Atkins [WHPO-1464])

Frankie Welch found her scarf-making services in great demand during the 1968 election season, on both the Republican and Democratic sides. "The 1968 political season impressed on Welch the power of conveying a message through fashion and she discovered her true calling, as a designer and promoter of signature scarves. . . . Her scarves—fashionable, collectible, lightweight, and easy to pack—proved to be the ideal promotional items."[34] Thanks to her network of well-connected boutique customers, she would eventually produce more than 4,000 political and corporate scarves. She remained in touch with Mrs. Johnson, whom she "knew very well," visiting her in Texas "several times."[35] She died in 2021, age 97.

Malcolm Starr, whose elegant but affordable evening looks were so popular with the political wives in the audience, went from success to success. At the National Symphony Ball on December 11, 1968, there were 13 identical Starr gowns; the following month, 27 women wore the same Starr gown to Nixon's inaugural ball.[36] But Pat Nixon turned to Harvey Berin for her yellow satin inaugural gown with its matching jacket embroidered in Swarovski crystals. Berin (or, rather, his designer Karen Stark) had been dressing Mrs. Nixon for years, having met then vice president Nixon in 1954, when he presented Berin with the National Cotton Award. (Judy Agnew, Rudi Gernreich's tablemate at the fashion show, became Second Lady.) In 1973, for her husband's second inauguration, Nixon went with a beaded turquoise gown by another Johnson favorite, Adele Simpson. George Halley and Luba Marks—two designers who "could hardly be more different"—were both honored with their first Coty Awards in July 1968; Oscar de la Renta received his second.[37] George Stavropoulos's flowing chiffon goddess gowns only grew in popularity during the disco decade, combining sensual elegance with ethnic-inspired exoticism. In 2014, decades after the designer's death, Lady Gaga was photographed wearing a vintage Stavropoulos gown in New York.

But other designers in the show did not fare so well. Rudi Gernreich's spring 1968 collection would be his last; he closed his company, though he continued to design on and off. Monte Sano would go out of business in 1969, and Sarmi shortly thereafter. In 1972, Larry Aldrich closed his company to concentrate on his art collecting and philanthropy. John Moore received a generous inheritance from his lover, Norman Norell, when he died in 1972; Moore soon retired and moved back to Alice, Texas, to run his family's antiques business.[38] Consumer indifference to the midi skirt forced many of its biggest proponents out of business by the early '70s; Chester Weinberg won the Coty Award in 1970, only to face bankruptcy in 1974. Weinberg and Gayle Kirkpatrick would eventually die of AIDS-related illnesses; John Kloss died by suicide amid financial problems, while lung cancer claimed the lives of Bill Blass, Rudi Gernreich, William Travilla,

The Johnsons welcome the Nixons to the White House on Inauguration Day, January 20, 1969. (Richard Nixon Presidential Library and Museum [WHPO-0023-19A])

and a number of the other designers. (After all, smoking was so common in the 1960s that the White House handed out branded matchbooks, and cigarettes were typical props in designer's publicity headshots.) The fashion industry mourned the untimely loss of Nina Hyde to breast cancer in 1990, at just 57 years old.

As for Mrs. Johnson, the politics of fashion continued to confound her right up to her last day in the White House. In early December, Liz Carpenter learned that Pat Nixon would wear a red dress for her husband's inauguration ceremony. Mrs. Johnson vented to her diary: "Sometime last week I had finally made the decision on the loveliest swatch of red wool for a coat and dress ensemble to be bought through I. Magnin. This must be canceled of course and we must start all over. And quick." A few weeks later, she lamented: "Alas, this costume has been plagued with bad luck from the beginning. First I decided on red only to discover that Mrs. Nixon's costume would be red, then I switched to yellow—too late, the sample they had shown me was no longer available on the market." She settled on a "peach pink wool coat and dress and a lovely fur helmet and muff."[39]

Wardrobe concerns—and frigid weather—notwithstanding, the day of the inauguration was one of the happiest of her life. "The one person in town who seemed unrestrainedly happy was Lady Bird Johnson, the retiring President's lady," the *New York Times* observed. "Wearing a coat of pale peach, she was animated and radiant throughout her husband's last ceremonial appearance as President. Her smile has never been freer. Mrs. Johnson, of course, has not lost a President, but gained a husband."[40]

That was not all she gained. As she prepared to leave the White House, Mrs. Johnson reflected on "the world of clothes which I have discovered these last five years. Perhaps actually I've been seduced into it."[41] Even *Women's Wear Daily* was won over in the end. "You could hardly call Lady Bird a fashion leader, but in those five years in the White House she's learned her fashion lessons well."[42] Though she may have been a reluctant pupil at times, her journey from "froufrou" to the best-dressed list—capped by a meaningful public tribute to the American fashion industry—represented an impressive learning curve. "'Discover America' was the show's title," the *Baltimore Sun* reported, "but it might well have been subtitled, 'Lady Bird Johnson's Changing Fashion Image.'"[43]

A final and more philosophical reason why the White House fashion experiment was never repeated was inadvertently suggested by Mrs. Orville Freeman, the wife of the secretary of agriculture, who said after the show: "It makes you itch to have more of a private life to wear these things. Girls in public life just have to be so careful about what we wear."[44] This is especially true of the First Lady. "Fashion starts at the White House," said Nina Hyde. "Front-page news makes front-page fashion. If a woman is going to be in the public eye, other women are influenced by what she wears."[45]

If there is one overarching fashion rule for First Ladies, it is to buy American-made clothes. The tradition dates back to George Washington's inauguration suit, which he had made by a New York tailor from painstakingly sourced Connecticut-woven broadcloth. First Ladies including Mary Todd Lincoln, Caroline Harrison, Frances Cleveland, and Edith Roosevelt made very public displays of purchasing American-made clothes, textiles, and furnishings. Though Mollie Parnis professed that "things shouldn't go out-of-date overnight," she urged her most prominent clients not just to buy American-made clothes but to buy new clothes *every season.* When Mamie Eisenhower insisted on wearing two-year-old dresses, Parnis told her: "It's a little like driving a 1955 Cadillac around Washington. You just can't *do* it. It would be bad for our industry."[46] Jackie Kennedy famously bent the buy-American rule, wearing authorized, line-for-line copies of French couture purchased from the New York boutique Chez Ninon. But her stylish example ultimately boosted the American fashion industry's reputation and bottom line. As Second Lady, Pat Nixon kept careful records of what she wore for public appearances, so as not to repeat herself—a practice adopted by Mrs. Johnson, who learned to keep up with fashion as a way of diverting the media's focus to things she considered more important. "You are on stage so much that your clothes go out of style all the time," Liz Carpenter reflected. "She didn't want clothes to devour her."[47] Rosalynn Carter brought a sewing machine to the White House, giving "Made in

America" a do-it-yourself spin. When Horst P. Horst arrived to shoot her portrait for *Vogue*, the hem of her skirt was so uneven that he had to disguise it in the photos.[48] Seventh Avenue breathed a sigh of relief when glamorous former actress Nancy Reagan replaced Carter as First Lady.

Many First Ladies since have occasionally donned foreign designers for State Dinners or on overseas trips, in tribute to their guests or hosts. But when a First Lady patronizes a foreign designer without a good excuse, the American media—and fashion industry—has tended to treat it as high treason. In 2011, the Council of Fashion Designers of America (CFDA)— founded by Eleanor Lambert—actually issued a press release criticizing Michelle Obama for wearing a gown by British designer Alexander Mc-Queen to a State Dinner in honor of the Chinese president, Hu Jintao. (A Chinese designer, presumably, would have been acceptable.) CFDA president Diane von Furstenberg wrote that Obama "has been wonderful at promoting our designers, so we were surprised and a little disappointed not to be represented for this major state dinner." And CFDA executive director Steve Kolb added that supporting American fashion was part of the president and First Lady's duty to spotlight "America, American jobs, American industry, American innovation."[49]

As Seventh Avenue has moved manufacturing overseas, buying American has become increasingly difficult; during the Clinton and Bush administrations, First Ladies tended to stick a few tried-and-true designers, like Bill Blass, Oscar de la Renta, Ralph Lauren, and Arnold Scaasi. Mrs. Obama intentionally highlighted the work of young American fashion and jewelry designers, particularly immigrants and designers of color, and mixed inexpensive labels with high-end pieces. Of President and Mrs. Trump's many deviations from presidential precedent, one of the most unremarked is their complete disregard of the perceived duty to wear American-made fashion. President Trump and his daughter Ivanka openly promoted their made-in-China clothing lines while trumpeting "American First" policies; Melania Trump, a Slovenian-born former fashion model, chose American designers for her Inauguration Day wardrobe but largely eschewed them afterward, a lapse perhaps masked by her relatively infrequent public appearances.

Despite this long-standing expectation of buying American, the Washington establishment continues to perceive fashion as "decidedly unserious," in *Vogue* editor Anna Wintour's words. When Mrs. Obama held a fashion study day at the White House in October 2014, she was careful to frame it as an "education workshop" for design students, though industry luminaries like Zac Posen, Tracy Reese, Philip Lim, Diane von Furstenberg, and Wintour were among the speakers. This "acknowledgment of the growing value and profile of the fashion industry"—a profile Obama had been instrumental in raising—drew predictable raves from those in the industry.

As if already anticipating the kinds of complaints Mrs. Johnson received, however, Mrs. Obama arrived armed with statistics on the fashion industry's economic impact, and the workshop included sessions on entrepreneurship and wearable technology as well as draping and inspiration. In addition to critical darlings like Posen and Lela Rose, there were representatives from mass-market success stories like J. Crew and Spanx. The *New York Times* account of the event made a point of noting that the First Lady had hosted a similar event for the film community the previous year.[50]

Michelle Obama with tailor Rory Duffy and students in the State Dining Room during the Fashion Education Workshop she hosted on October 9, 2014 (NARA)

In 1968, apparel was America's fourth largest industry and could not be ignored. As it declined in the 1970s and '80s, the propaganda value of fashion waned, and it became a political liability instead. Nancy Reagan was sharply criticized for buying expensive designer clothes and equally castigated when she accepted them for free. Hillary Clinton's pantsuits became a punchline during her presidential campaign, but they also telegraphed her transition from skirted First Lady to suited candidate. Mrs. Obama and Mrs. Trump were alternately hailed as inspirational fashion icons and blasted as free-spending fashion victims. And though Americans spent $35.3 billion on clothing and accessories in 2019, an estimated 95 percent of American clothing companies now manufacture their goods overseas, often in third-world sweatshops plagued by accidents and human rights violations. The impact of the COVID-19 pandemic on clothing production and consumption has yet to be calculated, but it is clear that its effects will be devastating, demanding careful reckoning and rebuilding. As fashion rises from the ashes, perhaps it's time for the industry to "Discover America" again.

Acknowledgments

Like so many adventures down research rabbit holes, this book began as a footnote in an entirely different book, in this case a biography of fashion designer Chester Weinberg. The captivating story of the one and only White House fashion show quickly took over that project, which remains in progress.

I wouldn't have made it very far down the rabbit hole without the generous support of the Lyndon Baines Johnson Foundation, which awarded me two Moody Research Grants to travel to the Lyndon Baines Johnson Presidential Library in Austin, where I found records of the fashion show in a wide range of media, miraculously intact and untouched. The team of archivists and curators were so helpful, even though I made the mistake of arriving wearing a "muley" dress that LBJ would have hated. I am grateful to Barbara Cline, Ian Frederick-Rothwell, Sara Nezamabadi, Renée Bair, Chris Banks, Lauren Gerson, Claudia Anderson, Regina Greenwell, Margaret Harman, Stephanie Savage, and Anne Wheeler for helping me navigate a treasure trove of material. The transcript of Lady Bird Johnson's oral diary was completed as I was writing this book and proved invaluable. Along with many other historians of the Johnson White House, I am indebted to those who supported and executed this monumental undertaking.

Ashley Callahan and Annette Becker generously shared their work on Frankie Welch and Mollie Parnis, respectively; it was a pleasure to swap ideas, images, and references with such insightful and hilarious colleagues. Another friend and colleague, Dennita Sewell, unwittingly transformed this project when she casually mentioned that she knew someone who had modeled in the fashion show. I am so grateful to her for putting me in touch with Cheryl "Sherry" Thomas. I was delighted to learn that Sherry not only kept in touch with her colleagues from her modeling days at Mannequin, but they got together for reunions! Bonnie Pfeifer Evans, Marcy Forrest, Jenny Chillcott Garrigues, Lynda Hatch, Fran Healy, Renée Hunter, and Peggy Parke Mathieu enthusiastically shared their memories and mementoes with me and brought to life a bygone world of fashion modeling. Their unique perspective on the fashion show added an entirely new dimension to this book. And it was a great privilege to interview two legendary women, China Machado and Bess Abell, before their deaths; even in their eighties, they were every bit as charming, funny, and feisty as you would expect.

Although many of the fashion show's organizers and participants are no longer alive, some of their descendants kindly shared images and information with a random stranger on the internet. I thank Peggy Welch Williams, Genie Welch Leisure, Peter Stavropoulos, Roy and Jeanie Campbell Petersen, Sandy Campbell, Sequoyah Hunter-Cuyjet, and Bob Knudsen. Sharon Francis, Deanna Littell, Arun Nevader, and Lynda Johnson Robb also lent valuable assistance.

I am so grateful to all the librarians, archivists, curators, and representatives of picture agencies who went above and beyond to provide information and images for this book in the midst of a global pandemic, when many of them were working from home. In addition to the LBJ Library staff, I owe special thanks to Kaitlyn Crain Enriquez at the National Archives and Records Administration, Ryan Pettigrew at the Nixon Library, Marian Ann Montgomery at Texas Tech University, Sara Hume at Kent State Museum, Edith Serkownek at the Kent State Fashion Library, Kate Medicus in Special Collections at the Kent State University Libraries, Eunice Haugen at the Goldstein Museum of Design, Kristina Haughland at the Philadelphia Museum of Art, Julie Burns at the DC Public Library, and Kevin Jones, Christina Johnson, Leigh Wishner, and Joanna Abijaoude at the Fashion Institute of Design and Merchandising Museum and Galleries, the home of Rudi Gernreich's archive.

At Kent State University Press, Susan Wadsworth-Booth, Jennifer Mower, Mary D. Young, Christine Brooks, Darryl Crosby, and Erin Holman patiently and painstakingly wove together all the strands of this visually and thematically complex book.

Although I have attempted to identify all the models, designers, and others shown in this book's images, even the models I interviewed had trouble recognizing themselves under all the hats, hairpieces, and false eyelashes. Similarly, every effort has been made to trace the photographers and copyright holders. Please contact the Kent State University Press for any additional information.

Portions of this research were published on *Slate.com* and *Politico.com*, and I thank those sites for allowing me to reproduce it here. I am also indebted to *Ornament*, where I first wrote about Mary Quant, and to my colleagues at the Costume Colloquium in Florence, Italy, where I presented an early version of this project.

This book was researched and written over some of the most turbulent years in American political history; comparisons to 1968 were frequent and accurate. For keeping me sane during "these hellish days," I am grateful to my friend and longtime editor at *Ornament*, the late Carolyn L. E. Benesh, to whom this book is dedicated. Carolyn, an eyewitness to the turmoil of the late 1960s, had a deep appreciation of the meaning and importance of fashion as political and personal expression, and I miss her wit and wisdom terribly.

Notes

Preface

1. Mary Quant, *Quant by Quant: The Autobiography of Mary Quant* (London: Victoria & Albert Museum, 2018), 156.
2. Marylin Bender, "Pop Fashion: Don't Count It Out," *New York Times*, Feb. 17, 1967.

1. The First Lady

1. Patricia Griffith, "Mamie Accepts Antiques: Early American Rug Is Late," *Washington Post*, June 30, 1960.
2. Fletcher Knebel, "Hopeful's Wife Runs Empire," *Los Angeles Times*, Mar. 1, 1960.
3. Lady Bird Audio Diary Transcripts, Nov. 22, 1963, p. 7, LBJ Library, Austin, TX (hereafter cited as Audio Diary).
4. "Mrs. Lyndon B. Johnson," *Women's Wear Daily*, Nov. 25, 1963.
5. Valentine Lawford, "Fashions in Living: A Garden of American History at the White House," *Vogue*, Feb. 1, 1967, 213.
6. Audio Diary, Mar. 9, 1967, 1–2.
7. "The Metamorphosis of Lady Bird; or, How I Learned to Stop Worrying and Love the White House," *Women's Wear Daily*, Oct. 14, 1968.
8. Marie Smith, "Another Veep from Blue Grass State?," *Washington Post*, Feb. 7, 1960.
9. "Eye," Women's Wear Daily, Oct. 15, 1963; "Mrs. Lyndon B. Johnson," Women's Wear Daily, Nov. 25, 1963.
10. Audio Diary, Oct. 11, 1967, 2.
11. Michael L. Gillette, *Lady Bird Johnson: An Oral History* (New York: Oxford Univ. Press, 2012), 188.
12. "The Eyes of Fashion Are upon Her," *Women's Wear Daily*, Nov. 27, 1963; "Washington Held Ready for A 'Little Something,'" *Women's Wear Daily*, Nov. 8, 1961; "Mrs. Lyndon B. Johnson," *Women's Wear Daily*, Nov. 25, 1963.
13. Virginia Lee Warren, "Mrs. Johnson Selects Style, Not Designer," *New York Times*, Aug. 28, 1964.
14. Transcript, Stanley Marcus Oral History Interview, Nov. 3, 1969, by Joe B. Frantz, AC75-16, pp. 6, 4, 3, LBJ Library.
15. Transcript, Bess Abell Oral History Interview I, May 28, 1969, by T. H. Baker, p. 13, LBJ Library.
16. "Eye," *Women's Wear Daily*, May 22, 1964.
17. Abell Oral History I, 13.
18. Marcus Oral History, 5.
19. Letter, Clara Treyz Geisler to Ashton Gonella, Nov. 22, 1964, "Simpson, Adele (Only)," White House Social Files, Alpha File, Box 1865, LBJ Library.

20. Abell Oral History I, 13.
21. Transcript, Mollie Parnis Oral History Interview, Oct. 13, 1983, by Michael L. Gillette, AC 84-49, p. 5, LBJ Library.
22. Abell Oral History I, 13.
23. Audio Diary, May 11, 1967, 1.
24. Jan Jarboe Russell, *Lady Bird: A Biography of Mrs. Johnson* (New York: Scribner, 2016), 122–23.
25. Marcus Oral History, 4.
26. Audio Diary, May 7, 1965, 1; Apr. 28, 1964, 4.
27. Rosemary Feitelberg, "Remembering Lady Bird," *Women's Wear Daily*, July 12, 2007; "Eye," *Women's Wear Daily*, May 22, 1964.
28. Warren, "Mrs. Johnson Selects Style, Not Designer."
29. "The Eyes of Fashion Are upon Her"; "Mrs. Lyndon B. Johnson."
30. Marcus Oral History, 19.
31. "People Are Talking About . . . Mrs. Lyndon Baines Johnson," *Vogue*, May 1, 1964, 147.
32. Audio Diary, Mar. 3, 1964, 2.
33. "Eye," *Women's Wear Daily*, Jan. 8, 1964; "Loud Liz: The National Mouth," *Women's Wear Daily*, Nov. 24, 1967.
34. Audio Diary, Jan. 8, 1965, 2.
35. Marcus Oral History, 16; "Eye," *Women's Wear Daily*, Dec. 26, 1963.
36. Audio Diary, Feb. 22, 1967, 2.
37. Audio Diary, Nov. 22, 1963, 6.
38. Gillette, *Lady Bird Johnson*, 282.
39. Audio Diary, Nov. 22, 1963, 6.
40. *Women's Wear Daily*, Feb. 13, 1961.
41. Audio Diary, Oct. 31, 1966, 11.
42. "Mrs. Lyndon B. Johnson"; Feitelberg, "Remembering Lady Bird."
43. Audio Diary, Nov. 26, 1963, 3.
44. "The Eyes of Fashion Are upon Her."
45. "Oral History Project of the Fashion Industries: Fashion Institute of Technology, Eleanor Lambert," interview by Phyllis Feldkamp, Dec. 8, 1977, 43, Special Collections and Library, Fashion Institute of Technology, New York.
46. Audio Diary, Sept. 15, 1965, 2; Feb. 15, 1968, 3; Jan. 23, 1966, 7.
47. Audio Diary, Oct. 29, 1966, 9; Aug. 22, 1967, 5.
48. Audio Diary, Feb. 13, 1968, 1.
49. Audio Diary, Oct. 11, 1967, 2; June 15, 1964, 1; Apr. 7, 1965, 1; "The Eyes of Fashion Are upon Her."
50. "White House Inspiration for Fashion," *Lawton (OK) Constitution and Morning Press*, Oct. 30, 1966.
51. Audio Diary, Aug. 6, 1965, 1; Sept. 9, 1964, 1; Feb. 22, 1967, 2.
52. Audio Diary, Jan. 21, 1964, 1; Jan. 28, 1964, 1; Jan. 29, 1964, 1; Jan. 27, 1965, 1.
53. Transcript, Elizabeth "Liz" Carpenter, Oral History Interview V, Feb. 2, 1971, by Joe B. Frantz, p. 28, LBJ Library.
54. Bernadine Morris, "The Nixons' Fashion Choices," *New York Times*, Jan. 15, 1969.
55. Audio Diary, Aug. 3, 1967, 2.
56. Gillette, *Lady Bird Johnson*, 354.
57. Audio Diary, Jan. 29, 1964, 1; Jan. 28, 1964, 1.
58. Audio Diary, Apr. 25, 1964, 1; Apr. 28, 1964, 4; Aug. 4, 1964, 3; Jan. 29, 1964, 1; Jan. 5, 1965, 1–2.
59. "First Lady Selects Spring Wardrobe," *New York Times*, Mar. 25, 1966.
60. "First Lady Selects Spring Wardrobe."
61. Abell Oral History I, 14.
62. "Eye," *Women's Wear Daily*, Nov. 4, 1963.
63. Audio Diary, Aug. 3, 1967, 1–2.
64. Martha Weinman, "First Ladies—in Fashion, Too?," *New York Times*, Sept. 11, 1960.
65. "Eye," *Women's Wear Daily*, Dec. 26, 1963.
66. Abell Oral History I, 14.
67. Audio Diary, Nov. 14, 1967, 6; Apr. 8, 1968, 11.
68. Abell Oral History I, 12.
69. Parnis Oral History, 3–4, 22.
70. Audio Diary, May 11, 1967, 1; Jan. 27, 1964, 1; Feb. 22, 1967, 1; Aug. 3, 1967, 2; May 7, 1965, 1.
71. "Mrs. Lyndon B. Johnson"; "The Eyes of Fashion Are upon Her."
72. Caroline Rennolds Milbank, *New York Fashion: The Evolution of American Style* (New York: Harry N. Abrams, 1989), 204.
73. Audio Diary, July 2, 1964, 1; May 15, 1968, 5; June 6, 1965, 7; Milbank, *New York Fashion*, 211.
74. Bess Abell, telephone interview, Nov. 12, 2014, by Kimberly Chrisman-Campbell.
75. Abell Oral History I, 13.

76. Audio Diary, Jan. 27, 1966, 1–2; May 18, 1967, 3.
77. Abell interview.
78. Audio Diary, Jan. 5, 1965, 2.
79. Audio Diary, Apr. 4, 1968, 4.
80. Audio Diary, Jan. 11, 1965, 3; Feb. 22, 1967, 1; Mar. 17, 1966, 9.
81. Marcus Oral History, 7.
82. Audio Diary, Jan. 5, 1965, 1.
83. "Eye," *Women's Wear Daily*, May 22, 1964; "People Are Talking About . . . Mrs. Lyndon Baines Johnson," 147; Knebel, "Empire."
84. "White House Inspiration for Fashion."
85. Audio Diary, June 17, 1965, 15.
86. Audio Diary, Mar. 17, 1966.
87. Marcus Oral History, 8.
88. Audio Diary, July 22, 1966, 1; June 2, 1966, 2.
89. Letter, Dorothea Anderson to Lady Bird Johnson, Sept. 8, 1964, and Letter, James McIntosh to Lady Bird Johnson, Aug. 1, both in "Dress (Dresses) (only) 1966–69," White House Social Files, Box 695, LBJ Library.
90. Letter, Bess Abell to Hannah Tanb, Mar. 18, 1964, "Fashion Show (Only)," White House Social Files, Alpha File, Box 767, LBJ Library.
91. Letter, Bess Abell to Florence G. Swift, Sept. 2, 1964, "Dress (Dresses) (only) 1963–65," White House Social Files, Alpha File, Box 695, LBJ Library.
92. Letter, Bess Abell to Mr. and Mrs. Edward Allston Jr., Mar. 11, 1964, "Dress (Dresses) (only) 1963–65," White House Social Files, Alpha File, Box 695, LBJ Library.
93. "Our Adventuresome First Lady," *Women's Wear Daily*, Mar. 23, 1966.
94. Audio Diary, June 2, 1966, 5; Mar. 9, 1967, 1–2.
95. "Our Adventuresome First Lady."
96. Audio Diary, Dec. 28, 1966, 5; Jan. 6, 1967, 3.
97. Audio Diary, Apr. 27, 1967, 5; Feb. 14, 1967, 3; Sept. 19, 1967, 1; Oct. 17, 1967, 1.
98. Joann Harris, "White House Puts On Fashions," *Baltimore Sun*, Mar. 10, 1968.
99. Audio Diary, Oct. 11, 1967, 2.

2. The Committee

1. Winzola McLendon and Scottie Smith, *Don't Quote Me! Washington Newswomen and the Power Society* (New York: Dutton, 1970), 146.
2. John Dickerson, *On Her Trail: My Mother, Nancy Dickerson, TV News' First Woman Star* (New York: Simon & Schuster, 2006), 207; Eleanor Lambert, "Nancy Dickerson Tops Writer's Best Dressed List," *Palm Beach Post*, Jan. 8, 1967.
3. Lady Bird Audio Diary Transcripts, Apr. 2, 1966, p. 9, Apr. 3, 1966, p. 8, LBJ Library, Austin, TX (hereafter cited as Audio Diary).
4. Transcript, Nancy Dickerson Oral History Interview, Aug. 11, 1972, by Joe B. Frantz, AC 80-5, p. 35, LBJ Library.
5. Dickerson, *On Her Trail*, 176.
6. "The Eyes of Fashion Are upon Her," *Women's Wear Daily*, Nov. 27, 1963; Dickerson Oral History, 35.
7. Audio Diary, Jan. 4, 1969, 6.
8. "Beauty Checkout," *Vogue*, Feb. 15, 1966, 26.
9. Bess Abell, telephone interview, Nov. 12, 2014, by Kimberly Chrisman-Campbell.
10. "Capital Summer," *Women's Wear Daily*, Aug. 18, 1961.
11. Michael L. Gillette, *Lady Bird Johnson: An Oral History* (New York: Oxford Univ. Press, 2012), 240.
12. Gillette, *Lady Bird Johnson*, 240, 241.
13. "Fashion Show (Only)," White House Social Files, Alpha File, Box 767, LBJ Library.
14. "The Eye," *Women's Wear Daily*, Mar. 21, 1962.
15. Audio Diary, Sept. 20, 1966, 2.
16. Audio Diary, Sept. 20, 1966, 1.
17. "Ladybird Flies with Fashion," *Washington Post*, Sept. 19, 1966.
18. Audio Diary, Sept. 20, 1966, 2.
19. White House Naval Photographic Unit, "Faces of the West, MP 1039," LBJ Library, uploaded Aug. 26, 2015, YouTube video, 27:27, https://youtu.be/5UQnPaAwtEs; White House Naval Photographic Unit, "Outs Roll 2 of 2 from MP1039 (Faces of the West)," LBJ Library, uploaded June 17, 2014, YouTube video, 21:40, https://youtube /xUjqU2dNo6Y.
20. Audio Diary, Sept. 20, 1966, 2.

21. Letter, Lady Bird Johnson to the Honorable Warren Woodward, Sept. 9, 1966, "Trip (California) 9/20/66," White House Social Files, Alpha File, LBJ Library.

22. Letter, Bess Abell to Eleanor Lambert, Apr. 15, 1965, "Mrs. C. Wyatt (Nancy H.) Dickerson," White House Social Files, Alpha File, Box 665, LBJ Library.

23. H. Stanley Marcus, "Future of Fashion," *Fortune*, Nov. 1940, 81.

24. Amy Fine Collins, "The Lady, the List, the Legacy," *Vanity Fair*, Apr. 2004, 267.

25. "The American Chic," *Vogue*, Mar. 15, 1957, 93.

26. Phyllis Magidson et al., *Mod New York: Fashion Takes a Trip* (New York: Museum of the City of New York and the Monacelli Press, 2017), 9.

27. Collins, "The Lady, the List, the Legacy," 267.

28. Letter, Eleanor Lambert to Lady Bird Johnson, Feb. 2, 1966, and Letter, Eleanor Lambert to Bess Abell, Feb. 16, 1966, both in Lambert, "Miss Eleanor (Only)," White House Social Files, Alpha File, Box 1333, LBJ Library.

29. Eugenia Sheppard, "White House Sets First Style Show," *Los Angeles Times*, Feb. 21, 1968.

30. Letter, Nancy Dickerson to Bess Abell, Aug. 16, 1966, "Fashion Show (Only)," White House Social Files, Alpha File, Box 767, LBJ Library.

31. Audio Diary, July 15, 1966, 5.

32. Eugenia Sheppard, "Designer Norell Coordinates a Benefit Fashion Ballet," *Washington Post*, Aug. 15, 1966.

33. Letter, Nancy Dickerson to Lady Bird Johnson, Sept. 26, 1966, "Fashion Show (Only)," White House Social Files, Alpha File, Box 767, LBJ Library.

34. Abell interview.

35. Press release, Office of the Press Secretary to Mrs. Johnson, Feb. 28, 1968, "Fashion Show/Luncheon for Governor's Wives 2/29/68," White House Social Files, Liz Carpenter's Files, Box 46, LBJ Library.

36. "V.P. and D.D. Stroll on S.A.," *Women's Wear Daily*, Oct. 16, 1963.

37. "S.A. Firms Close Ranks to Keep out French Goods," *Women's Wear Daily*, Dec. 6, 1967.

38. Abell interview.

39. Eugenia Sheppard, "White House Sets First Style Show," *Los Angeles Times*, Feb. 21, 1968.

40. Lyndon B. Johnson, "Discover America Planning Week, Proclamation 3780. Dated April 15, 1967," *Weekly Compilation of Presidential Documents* 3, no. 16 (Washington, DC: Office of the Federal Register, National Archives and Records Service, Apr. 24, 1967), 642.

41. Press release, Office of the Press Secretary to Mrs. Johnson, Feb. 28, 1968.

42. Mary Strasburg, "See the USA—the Johnson Way," *Washington Post*, Feb. 24, 1968.

43. Gillette, *Lady Bird Johnson*, 357.

44. Dale McConathy, "Wife-Power," *Vogue*, June 1, 1971, 110.

45. Sharon Francis, telephone interview, Nov. 10, 2014, by Kimberly Chrisman-Campbell.

46. Frances Spatz Leighton, "It Looked Easy—but It Wasn't!," *Chicago Tribune*, May 5, 1968.

47. Joann Harris, "White House Puts On Fashions," *Baltimore Sun*, Mar. 10, 1968.

48. Valli Herman-Cohen, "Nancy White, 85; Edited Harper's Bazaar 1958–71," *Los Angeles Times*, May 31, 2002.

49. Douglas Martin, "Nancy White, 85, Dies; Edited Harper's Bazaar in the 60's," *New York Times*, May 29, 2002.

50. *Frederick (MD) News-Post*, Apr. 2, 1971, quoted in Kimberly Wilmot Voss and Lance Speere, "Fashion as Washington Journalism History: Eleni Epstein and Her Three Decades at the *Washington Star*," *Media History Monographs* 16, no. 3 (2013–14): 1–22, 5.

51. McLendon and Smith, *Don't Quote Me!*, 177.

52. "Dorothy LeSueur," *Washington Post*, July 3, 2009.

53. "Eye," *Women's Wear Daily*, Mar. 22, 1972.

54. Abell interview.

55. McLendon and Smith, *Don't Quote Me!*, 176.

56. Peg Zwecker, "Peg Says: Worthy House to Open Again," *Chicago Daily News*, Feb. 23, 1968.

57. Leighton, "It Looked Easy."

58. Marie Smith, "LBJ's Party Planner: She's Cruise Director for the Ship of State," *Washington Post*, May 7, 1967.

59. Undated, unsigned note, "White House Fashion Show, 2/29/1968 [1 of 3]," White

House Social Files, Bess Abell Files, Box 23, LBJ Library.

60. Myra MacPherson, "Governors' Wives 'Discover America in Style' at White House," *New York Times*, Mar. 1, 1968.

61. Zwecker, "Peg Says."

62. MacPherson, "Governors' Wives 'Discover America in Style.'"

63. Rubye Graham, "White House Holds First Fashion Show," *Philadelphia Inquirer*, Mar. 1, 1968.

64. Audio Diary, Sept. 13, 1967, 5.

65. Barbara Cloud, "Patriotism Style at First White House Fashion Show," *Pittsburgh Press*, Mar. 1, 1968; Letter, Lady Bird Johnson to George K. Payne, Mar. 11, 1968, "White House Fashion Show, 2/29/1968 [2 of 3]," White House Social Files, Bess Abell Files, Box 23, LBJ Library.

66. Memo, Curator's Office to Barbara Keehn, Feb. 27, 1968, "White House Fashion Show, 2/29/1968 [1 of 3]," White House Social Files, Bess Abell Files, Box 23, LBJ Library.

67. See Ashley Callahan, "Frankie Welch: Americana Fashion Specialist," *Ornament* 35, no. 1 (2011): 26–31.

68. Gay Pauley, "'Designing' Woman Works Both Sides," *Cincinnati Enquirer*, July 4, 1968.

69. Jennifer Levin, "Ready to Wear," *Pasatiempo*, Feb. 12, 2016, 36.

70. Eugenia Sheppard, "'Signature Scarfs' Designers' Delight," *Boston Globe*, Jan. 23, 1967.

71. Letter, Bess Abell to Barbara Kling, May 29, 1968, "Lane, F–K," White House Social Files, Alpha File, Box 1336, LBJ Library.

72. Abell interview.

73. Letter, Frankie Welch to Bess Abell, n.d., "White House Fashion Show, 2/29/1968 [2 of 3]," White House Social Files, Bess Abell Files, Box 23, LBJ Library.

74. Letter, Frankie Welch to Liz Carpenter, Feb. 9, 1968, "White House Fashion Show, 2/29/1968 [1 of 3]," White House Social Files, Bess Abell Files, Box 23, LBJ Library.

75. Eugenia Sheppard, "Fashion Has Its First Big Fling at the White House," *Los Angeles Times*, Mar. 4, 1968.

76. Letter, Frankie Welch to Liz Carpenter, Feb. 9, 1968, "White House Fashion Show,

2/29/1968 [1 of 3]," White House Social Files, Bess Abell Files, Box 23, LBJ Library.

77. Denver Public Library, Special Collections, Governor John Love Papers, Series 4, Personal/Ann Love, Box 7, FF10.

78. Letter, Frankie Welch to Liz Carpenter, Feb. 9, 1968, "White House Fashion Show, 2/29/1968 [1 of 3]," White House Social Files, Bess Abell Files, Box 23, LBJ Library.

79. Frances Cawthon, "Hometown Fetes Designer," *Atlanta Constitution*, Sept. 28, 1969.

80. Gay Pauley, "'Designing' Woman Works Both Sides," *Cincinnati Enquirer*, July 4, 1968; Meryle Secrest, "Reflections on a Recent Texas Trip," *Washington Post*, Apr. 14, 1968.

81. Letter, Frankie Welch to Bess Abell, Feb. 9, 1968, "Luncheon (Mrs. Johnson) (Governor's Wives)," White House Social Files, White House Social Entertainment, Box 109, LBJ Library; Eugenia Sheppard, "Fashion Has Its First Big Fling at the White House," *Los Angeles Times*, Mar. 4, 1968; Letter, Frankie Welch to Liz Carpenter, Feb. 9, 1968, "White House Fashion Show, 2/29/1968 [1 of 3]," White House Social Files, Bess Abell Files, Box 23, LBJ Library.

82. Letter, Frankie Welch to Bess Abell, Feb. 9, 1968, "Luncheon (Mrs. Johnson) (Governor's Wives)," White House Social Files, White House Social Entertainment, Box 109, LBJ Library.

83. Callahan, "Frankie Welch," 29.

84. Jo Ann Coker Harris, "N. C. Indians Influence Designer," *Charlotte Observer*, Aug. 8, 1968.

85. Myra MacPherson, "If You Think a Political Button Isn't Enough . . ." *New York Times*, June 20, 1968; Frankie Welch Collection photo, Rome Area History Center, GA (I am grateful to Ashley Callahan for the reference).

86. Letter, Bess Abell to Frankie Welch, Apr. 11, 1968, "Dress (Dresses) (only) 1966–69," White House Social Files, Alpha File, Box 695, LBJ Library.

87. Letter, Frankie letter to Bess Abell, Feb. 9, 1968, "Luncheon (Mrs. Johnson) (Governor's Wives)," White House Social Files, White House Social Entertainment, Box 109, LBJ Library.

88. MacPherson, "Governors' Wives 'Discover America in Style.'"

89. Sherry Thomas, telephone interview, May 14, 2015, by Kimberly Chrisman-Campbell.

90. Mary Strasburg, "See the USA—The Johnson Way," *Washington Post*, Feb. 24, 1968.

91. Sharon Francis, telephone interview, Nov. 7, 2014, by Kimberly Chrisman-Campbell.

92. Strasburg, "See the USA."

93. Notes on telephone conversation between Liz Carpenter and Eleanor Lambert, Feb. 21, 1968, "Governor's Wives—2/29/68," White House Social Files, Bess Abell Files, Box 23, LBJ Library.

94. Strasburg, "See the USA."

95. Audio Diary, Feb. 6, 1968, 6, 7; Feb. 15, 1968, 5.

96. "White House Fashion Show," *New York Times*, Feb. 22, 1968.

97. President's Daily Diary, Feb. 28, 1968, LBJ Library.

98. Memo, Bess Abell to the Garage, Feb. 26, 1968, "White House Fashion Show, 2/29/1968 [1 of 3]," White House Social Files, Bess Abell Files, Box 23, LBJ Library.

99. Leighton, "It Looked Easy."

100. Audio Diary, Feb. 28, 1968, 1.

101. Peg Zwecker, "Peg Says: White House Show a Hit," *Chicago Daily News*, Mar. 1, 1968.

102. Harris, "White House Puts On Fashions."

103. Lady Bird Johnson's Daily Diary, Feb. 28, 1968, LBJ Library.

104. Walter Pincus, "Remembering McNamara's Hope for Peace," *Washington Post*, July 7, 2009.

105. Audio Diary, Feb. 28, 1968, 4.

3. The Models

1. "Cherokee Alphabet," *Daily Independent* (Kannapolis, NC), Oct. 29, 1967.

2. "Lynda's Look-Alike Differs in Other Ways," *Fort Worth Star-Telegram*, Dec. 2, 1967.

3. "Lynda Bird's Double Unperturbed by Status," *Times-Advocate* (Escondido, CA), Dec. 13, 1967.

4. Dorothy LeSueur, "The Pleasure of Pretty Patterns," *Washington Post*, Feb. 16, 1969.

5. Bonnie Pfeifer Evans, telephone interview, Apr. 21, 2021, by Kimberly Chrisman-Campbell.

6. Memo, Carol Carlye to the Ushers, PRS, and Major Lanier, Feb. 28, 1968, "White House Fashion Show, 2/29/1968 [2 of 3]," White House Social Files, Bess Abell Files, Box 23, LBJ Library, Austin, TX.

7. Lady Bird Audio Diary Transcripts, Feb. 28, 1968, p. 5, LBJ Library (hereafter cited as Audio Diary).

8. Eugenia Sheppard, "'Papa San' Norell Brings Home the Girls," *Sunday Star-Bulletin & Advertiser* (Honolulu), Oct. 3, 1965.

9. Barbara Cloud, "Fashion Focus," *Pittsburgh Press*, Mar. 5, 1968.

10. Etta Froio, "Gillis MacGil, 85," *Women's Wear Daily*, Dec. 18, 2013.

11. Gloria Emerson, "A Baker's Dozen of Slim Beauties Set to Model High Fashions: New Agency Here Will Specialize in Showings," *New York Times*, Nov. 16, 1960.

12. Dorothea T. Apgar, "Top N. Y. Models Form Exclusive Club," *Wilmington News Journal*, July 26, 1961.

13. Sandra Sulenski, "Models Need Beauty AND Brains," *Decatur (IL) Daily Review*, Jan. 19, 1964; Kathy Larkin, "Focus on Two Young Girls Who Lead a Model Life," *Daily News* (New York), July 11, 1971.

14. Larkin, "Focus on Two Young Girls"; Emerson, "A Baker's Dozen of Slim Beauties."

15. Apgar, "Top N. Y. Models Form Exclusive Club."

16. Sulenski, "Models Need Beauty AND Brains."

17. Lynn Felder, "NC Native Made History as Black Model," *Asheville Citizen-Times*, July 28, 2014.

18. Froio, "Gillis MacGil, 85."

19. Marilyn Hoffman, "Gillis MacGil: From Top Fashion Model to Owner of a Model Agency," *Christian Science Monitor*, Feb. 24, 1983.

20. Apgar, "Top N. Y. Models Form Exclusive Club."

21. "Beauty Is . . . ," *Women's Wear Daily*, Sept. 26, 1968.

22. Bernadine Morris, "Housewives Who Slip Out of Aprons and Into Haute Couture," *New York Times*, Oct. 20, 1969.

23. Apgar, "Top N. Y. Models Form Exclusive Club."

24. Bill Cunningham, "A Sidewalk Fashion Show," *Chicago Tribune*, June 17, 1968.

25. Ellen Jacobson, "English Girl Emphasizes the New Trend in Models," *Morning Call* (Paterson, NJ), Sept. 3, 1966.

26. Eugenia Sheppard, "Designers Switch Models for That Just-Right Look," *Los Angeles Times*, May 21, 1968.

27. Jennifer Chillcott Garrigues, telephone interview, May 4, 2021, by Kimberly Chrisman-Campbell.

28. "Galanos Favors a Model Built 'Like a Snake,'" *New York Times*, Aug 11, 1964.

29. Bernadine Morris, "The Galanos Girls," *New York Times*, Dec. 26, 1966.

30. Lester Gaba, "Lester Gaba Looks at Display," *Women's Wear Daily*, Feb. 14, 1967.

31. Bender, *The Beautiful People*, 172.

32. Roberta Roesch, "Modeling Is More Hard Work Than Glamor," *Record* (Hackensack, NY), Dec. 14, 1969.

33. Peggy Parke Mathieu, telephone interview, July 6, 2017, by Kimberly Chrisman-Campbell.

34. Lynda Hatch, telephone interview, Apr. 19, 2021, by Kimberly Chrisman-Campbell.

35. Sherry Thomas, telephone interview, May 14, 2015, by Kimberly Chrisman-Campbell.

36. Bill Cunningham, "All of the Women at the Wedding," *Chicago Tribune*, Mar. 20, 1972; Bernadine Morris, "No False Eyelashes for Scarlett O'Hara," *New York Times*, Nov. 29, 1967.

37. Bernadine Morris, "Housewives Who Slip Out of Aprons and Into Haute Couture," *New York Times*, Oct. 20, 1969.

38. Enid Nemy, "Three Models: Fashion Is Their Job—and Their Hobby, Too," *New York Times*, Aug. 30, 1967.

39. Jacobson, "English Girl Emphasizes the New Trend."

40. Garrigues interview.

41. Vidal Sassoon, *Vidal: The Autobiography* (London: Pan Books, 2011), 172.

42. Gloria Emerson, "A Baker's Dozen of Slim Beauties."

43. Apgar, "Top N. Y. Models Form Exclusive Club."

44. Bernadine Morris, "Models Try Business World On for Size," *New York Times*, Oct. 23, 1971.

45. Marylin Bender, "Negro Role in Modeling Is Growing: Pattern Companies," *New York Times*, Sept. 5, 1964.

46. "Beauty Is . . . ," *Women's Wear Daily*, Sept. 26, 1968.

47. Felder, "NC Native Made History as Black Model."

48. Eleanor Lambert, "Twiggy? We Prefer Girly Models," *Charlotte Observer*, Apr. 2, 1967.

49. "Beauty Is . . . "

50. Karen B. Tancill, "Model Behavior," *Journal-Times* (Racine, WI), Oct. 24, 1968.

51. Felder, "NC Native Made History as Black Model."

52. Renée Hunter, telephone interview, May 19, 2021, by Kimberly Chrisman-Campbell.

53. Bernadine Morris, "Indian Story Told through Fashion," *New York Times*, Dec, 5, 1972.

54. "Beauty Is . . . ," *Women's Wear Daily*, Sept. 26, 1968.

55. Hunter interview.

56. Eugenia Sheppard, "Models Chosen for Just-Right Look," *Los Angeles Times*, May 21, 1968.

57. Bonnie Miller Rubin, "Sound Eating Habits Help Ex-Model Fight Creeping Pounds," *Minneapolis Star Tribune*, Aug. 25, 1977; Eugenia Sheppard, "Acres of Skin," *Hartford Courant*, Oct. 31, 1963.

58. Helen Hennessy, "Gernreich Shocks 'Em Again," *Town Talk* (Alexandria, LA), Oct. 8, 1966.

59. Larkin, "Focus on Two Young Girls."

60. Advertisement for US Rubber, *Vogue*, Sept. 1, 1965, 157.

61. May Okon, "A View from the East," *Daily News* (New York), Mar. 18, 1962.

62. Hunter interview.

63. Diane Costa, "Bill Blass: Fashion Designer for Individuals," *Times Herald* (Port Huron, MI), Nov. 14, 1967.

64. Laurena Pringle, "The Winans' in Hawaii after Family Wedding," *Detroit Free Press*, Jan. 21, 1968.

65. Hunter interview.

66. Lana Ellis, "Bill Blass Shows His Style," *Louisville Courier-Journal*, May 17, 1968.

67. Mathieu interview.
68. Jacobson, "English Girl Emphasizes the New Trend."
69. Hunter interview.
70. Nemy, "Three Models."
71. Thomas interview.
72. Mathieu interview.
73. Memo, Carol Carlyle to the Ushers Office, Feb. 26, 1968, "White House Fashion Show, 2/29/1968 [2 of 3]," White House Social Files, Bess Abell Files, Box 23, LBJ Library; Frances Lewine, "White House Fashion Show Held for Governor's Wives," *Spokane Daily Chronicle*, Mar. 4, 1968.
74. Frances Spatz Leighton, "It Looked Easy—but It Wasn't!," *Chicago Tribune*, May 5, 1968.
75. Mathieu interview.
76. Thomas interview.
77. China Machado, telephone interview, Nov. 12, 2014, by Kimberly Chrisman-Campbell.
78. Memo, Carol Carlye to the Ushers, PRS, and Major Lanier, Feb. 28, 1968, "White House Fashion Show, 2/29/1968 [2 of 3]," White House Social Files, Bess Abell Files, Box 23, LBJ Library.
79. Leighton, "It Looked Easy."
80. Hunter interview.
81. Thomas interview.
82. Eleni, "White House Fashion First Waves Flag for U.S. Travel," *Evening Star* (Washington, DC), Mar. 1, 1968. Eleni Epstein used her first name as her byline.
83. Leighton, "It Looked Easy."
84. Thomas interview.
85. Mathieu interview.
86. Eleni, "White House Fashion First Waves Flag for U.S. Travel," *Evening Star* (Washington, DC), Mar. 1, 1968.
87. Audio Diary, Feb. 28, 1968, 6, 7.
88. Kimberly Wilmot Voss and Lance Speere, "Fashion as Washington Journalism History: Eleni Epstein and Her Three Decades at the Washington Star," *Media History Monographs* 16, no. 3 (2013–14): 12.
89. Machado interview.
90. Mary Strasburg, "VIP Wives 'Discover America' . . . the White House Way," *Washington Post*, Mar. 1, 1968.
91. "Happening," *Washington Post*, Mar. 2, 1968.
92. Memo, Carol Carlyle to the Ushers Office, Feb. 26, 1968, "White House Fashion Show, 2/29/1968 [1 of 3]," White House Social Files, Bess Abell Files, Box 23, LBJ Library.
93. Mathieu interview.
94. Machado interview.
95. Lady Bird Johnson to Gilis MacGil, Mar. 6, 1968, "Fashion Show (Special)," White House Social Files, Alpha File, Box 768, LBJ Library.

4. The Guest List

1. Eugenia Sheppard, "Fashion Has Its First Big Fling at the White House," *Los Angeles Times*, Mar. 4, 1968.
2. Eleni, "White House Fashion First Waves Flag for U.S. Travel," *Evening Star* (Washington, DC), Mar. 1, 1968.
3. Lady Bird Audio Diary Transcripts, Aug. 15, 1967, p. 6; July 22, 1966, p. 1, LBJ Library, Austin, TX (hereafter cited as Audio Diary). There was no question of Luci attending the fashion show; at the time, she lived in Austin, Texas, and had an infant son. Deanna Littell, telephone interview, Aug. 3, 2021, by Kimberly Chrisman-Campbell.
4. Transcript, Bess Abell Oral History Interview II, June 13, 1969, by T. H. Baker, p. 7, LBJ Library.
5. "The Metamorphosis of Lynda Bird," *Women's Wear Daily*, Sept. 12, 1967.
6. George Hamilton and William Stadiem, *Don't Mind If I Do* (New York: Touchstone, 2008), 197, 194.
7. Audio Diary, Oct. 8, 1965, 6.
8. Marylin Bender, *The Beautiful People* (New York: Coward-McCann, 1967), 257
9. Audio Diary, Jan. 25, 1965, 3; June 5, 1967, 4; Dec. 5, 1967, 7; June 1, 1967, 6.
10. Myra MacPherson, "Governors' Wives 'Discover America in Style' at White House," *New York Times*, Mar. 1, 1968; Peg Zwecker, "Peg Says: White House Show a Hit," *Chicago Daily News*, Mar. 1, 1968; Audio Diary, Jan. 17, 1968.
11. Audio Diary, Dec. 24, 1967, 4.
12. "That Wedding . . . ," *Women's Wear Daily*, Dec. 11, 1967.

13. Audio Diary, Dec. 9, 1967.
14. Barbara Cloud, "Patriotism Style at First White House Fashion Show," *Pittsburgh Press*, Mar. 1, 1968.
15. Audio Diary, June 12, 1967, 1.
16. Katherine Harrington, "Historic Event, Washington Style," *Knickerbocker News* (Albany, NY), Mar. 1, 1968; Zwecker, "Peg Says"; MacPherson, "Governors' Wives 'Discover America in Style.'"
17. Mary Strasburg, "VIP Wives 'Discover America' . . . the White House Way," *Washington Post*, Mar. 1, 1968.
18. Sheppard, "Fashion Has Its First Big Fling at the White House."
19. Eugenia Sheppard, "Inside Fashion," *Women's Wear Daily*, Mar. 1, 1968.
20. Quoted in John Dickerson, *On Her Trail: My Mother, Nancy Dickerson, TV News' First Woman Star* (New York: Simon & Schuster, 2006), 221.
21. Rubye Graham, "White House Holds First Fashion Show," *Philadelphia Inquirer*, Mar. 1, 1968; Vera Glaser, "Happy Takes to White House," *Palm Beach Post*, Mar. 8, 1968.
22. Zwecker, "Peg Says."
23. MacPherson, "Governors' Wives 'Discover America in Style.'"
24. Sheppard, "Fashion Has Its First Big Fling at the White House."
25. Ruth Preston, "Talk about Clothes: Lunch at the White House," *New York Post*, Mar. 1, 1968.
26. Peggy Parke Mathieu, telephone interview, July 6, 2017, by Kimberly Chrisman-Campbell.
27. Eleni, "White House Fashion First Waves Flag for U.S. Travel."
28. Press list for fashion luncheon, "White House Fashion Show [1 of 3]," White House Social Files, Bess Abell Files, Box 23, LBJ Library.
29. Press List for Fashion Luncheon, "White House Fashion Show, 2/29/1968 [1 of 3]," White House Social Files, Bess Abell Files, Box 23, LBJ Library.
30. Kimberly Wilmot Voss and Lance Speere, "Fashion as Washington Journalism History: Eleni Epstein and Her Three Decades at the

Washington Star," *Media History Monographs* 16, no. 3 (2013–14): 1.
31. White House Naval Photographic Unit, *The President: February 1968*, MP893, LBJ Library, uploaded Jan. 9, 2013, YouTube video, 58:49, https://www.youtube.com/watch?v=39Fa6r19NF8.
32. MacPherson, "Governors' Wives 'Discover America in Style.'"

5. The Designers

1. Mary Strasburg, "Fashion Flies In with USA Labels," *Washington Post*, Feb. 29, 1968.
2. Peg Zwecker, "Peg Says: White House Show a Hit," *Chicago Daily News*, Mar. 1, 1968.
3. Rubye Graham, "White House Holds First Fashion Show," *Philadelphia Inquirer*, Mar. 1, 1968.
4. Virginia Lee Warren, "Mrs. Johnson Selects Style, Not Designer," *New York Times*, Aug. 28, 1964.
5. Lady Bird Johnson Audio Diary Transcripts, Jan. 5, 1965, 1; June 9, 1965, 1; Feb. 14, 1967, 3, LBJ Library, Austin, TX (hereafter cited as Audio Diary).
6. "Abe Schrader, 'Fashion King,' Dead at 100," *Times-Tribune*, July 13, 2001.
7. Strasburg, "Fashion Flies In."
8. Strasburg, "Fashion Flies In."
9. Bill Blass, *Bare Blass* (New York: HarperCollins, 2002), 20.
10. Blass, *Bare Blass*, 8, 11.
11. Bernadine Morris, "Weinberg Joins Designers-Turned-Businessmen," *New York Times*, Mar. 26, 1966.
12. Sarah Mower and Anna Wintour, *Oscar: The Style, Inspiration and Life of Oscar de la Renta* (New York: Assouline, 2002), 90.
13. Michael L. Gillette, *Lady Bird Johnson: An Oral History* (New York: Oxford Univ. Press, 2012), 240.
14. Wauhillau La Hay, "Governors' Wives Ooh and Ah As White House Scores First," *Memphis Press-Scimitar*, Mar. 2, 1968.
15. Audio Diary, Aug. 22, 1966, 9.
16. Memo, Bess Abell to Lady Bird Johnson, Feb. 28, 1968, "Luncheon (Mrs. Johnson)

(Governor's Wives) Thursday, February 29, 1968 at 1:00 pm," White House Social Files, White House Social Entertainment, Box 109, LBJ Library.

17. Zwecker, "Peg Says."

18. Eugenia Sheppard, "Fashion Has Its First Big Fling at the White House," *Los Angeles Times*, Mar. 4, 1968.

19. Audio Diary, Apr. 11, 1968, 7; July 19, 1966, 1.

20. Myra MacPherson, "Governors' Wives 'Discover America in Style' at White House," *New York Times*, Mar. 1, 1968.

21. "White House Fashion First Waves Flag for U.S. Travel," *Evening Star*, Mar. 1, 1968.

22. Mary Strasburg, "VIP Wives 'Discover America' . . . The White House Way," *Washington Post*, Mar. 1, 1968; Sheppard, "Fashion Has Its First Big Fling at the White House"; Barbara Cloud, "The First and Last White House Fashion Show," *Pittsburgh Post-Gazette*, Mar. 25, 2006; Zwecker, "Peg Says."

23. Bernadine Morris, *The Fashion Makers* (New York: Random House, 1978), 209.

24. *Chicago Daily News*, Mar. 1, 1968.

25. Joann Harris, "White House Puts On Fashions," *Baltimore Sun*, Mar. 10, 1968; Strasburg, "VIP Wives 'Discover America'"; La Hay, "Governors' Wives Ooh and Ah As White House Scores First."

26. Zwecker, "Peg Says."

27. Judy Klemesrud, "Bill Blass From Head to Toe," *New York Times*, Nov. 7, 1967.

28. Winzola McClendon and Scottie Smith, *Don't Quote Me! Washington Newswomen and the Power Society* (New York: Dutton, 1970), 177.

29. Rick Beyer and Elizabeth Sayles, *The Ghost Army of World War II: How One Top-Secret Unit Deceived the Enemy with Inflatable Tanks, Sound Effects, and Other Audacious Fakery* (New York: Princeton Architectural Press, 2015), 231.

30. L.E.B.H., "Man à la Mode," *Saturday Evening Post*, Apr. 6, 1968, 30.

31. Blass, *Bare Blass*, 6.

32. James Brady, "Ego, Libido, Genius, Chicanery: The Inside Story of Fashion," *New York Magazine*, Nov. 25, 1974, 71.

33. "The Beautiful People," *Vogue*, June 1, 1968, 154–61.

34. Letter, Lady Bird Johnson to Adolfo, Mar. 13, 1968, "Adolfo (Only)," White House Social Files, Alpha File, Box 6, LBJ Library.

35. Audio Diary, Jan. 5, 1965, 1.

36. Morris, *Fashion Makers*, 13, 16.

37. Bernadine Morris, "The Galanos Girls," *New York Times*, Dec. 26, 1966.

38. Audio Diary, Apr. 14, 1964, 4.

39. "Lady Bird Shies Away From Black," *Indianapolis News*, Aug. 8, 1967; Audio Diary, Aug. 3, 1967; Apr. 27, 1967; Feb. 15, 1968, 2.

40. Transcript, Stanley Marcus Oral History Interview, Nov. 3, 1969, by Joe B. Frantz, AC 75-16, p. 7, LBJ Library.

41. Warren, "Mrs. Johnson Selects Style, Not Designer."

42. Eleanor Lambert, *World of Fashion, People, Places, Resources* (New York: R. R. Bowker, 1976), 252.

43. Morris, *Fashion Makers*, 198.

44. Bernadine Morris, "Seventh Avenue's Campaigners for the Fashion Rights of Women," *New York Times*, Apr. 24, 1967.

45. Transcript, Mollie Parnis Oral History Interview, Oct. 13, 1983, by Michael L. Gillette, AC 84-49, p. 12, LBJ Library.

46. Letter, Mollie Parnis to Mrs. Johnson, Dec. 2, 1963, "Parnis, Miss Mollie (Only)," White House Social Files, Alpha File, Box 1607, LBJ Library.

47. Diana Lurie, "Close-Up: When Mollie Parnis Thinks a Dress Will Sell, It Goes," *LIFE*, June 17, 1966, 47.

48. Morris, *Fashion Makers*, 170.

49. Audio Diary, Jan. 17, 1967, 5; May 7, 1965, 1; Jan. 17, 1967, 5; Mar. 28, 1966. She wore the white Parnis dress in a 1967 publicity picture by presidential photographer Yoichi Okamato.

50. Parnis Oral History, 7, 9, 10, 4; transcript, Nancy Dickerson Oral History Interview, Aug. 11, 1972, by Joe B. Frantz, AC 80-5, p. 8, LBJ Library.

51. Audio Diary, Feb. 13, 1968, 1.

52. Marylin Bender, *The Beautiful People* (New York: Coward-McCann, 1967), 70–71.

53. Audio Diary, Nov. 8, 1967, 10, 13.

54. Caroline Reynolds Milbank, *New York Fashion: The Evolution of American Style* (New York: Harry N. Abrams, 1989), 212.

55. Lambert, *World of Fashion*, 238–39.

56. Bernadine Morris, "From Gernreich: The Belted Neckline," *New York Times*, May 10, 1967.

57. Bernadine Morris, "George P. Stavropoulos, Designer of Chiffon Classics, Is Dead at 70," *New York Times*, Dec. 11, 1990.

58. Audio Diary, May 27, 1968, 4; Feb. 22, 1967, 2; Nov. 21, 1968, 10.

59. George Stavropoulos, "Real Woman Coming into Focus," *Philadelphia Inquirer*, Feb. 26, 1968.

60. Peter Stavropoulos, telephone interview, May 17, 2021, by Kimberly Chrisman-Campbell.

61. Joan Nielsen McHale, "Costume Jewelry Is Respectable," *Miami News*, Feb. 20, 1968.

62. Letter, Bess Abell to Kenneth Jay Lane, Jan. 10, 1968, Letter, Bess Abell to Nina Hyde, Jan. 10, 1968, both in "Lane, F–K," White House Social Files, Alpha File, Box 1336, LBJ Library.

63. Morris, "Galanos Girls."

64. Mildred Finger, "Oral History Project of the Fashion Industries: Fashion Institute of Technology, David Evins: Shoe Designer and Manufacturer," 19, Nov. 16, 1982, Special Collections and Library, Fashion Institute of Technology, New York.

65. Carol Bjorkman, "Carol Says," *Women's Wear Daily*, Oct. 16, 1963.

66. "Halley's Comet," *Women's Wear Daily*, June 30, 1967.

67. Bernadine Morris, "No False Eyelashes for Scarlett O'Hara," *New York Times*, Nov. 29, 1967.

68. Marian Christy, "George Halley Hits Jackpot," *Boston Globe*, Dec. 28, 1969.

69. "'Rolls Royce' of Knitwear Purrs On," *Women's Wear Daily*, Apr. 4, 1967; "Jazzier Styles, Brighter Tints Win Knit Converts," *Women's Wear Daily*, Feb. 27, 1967.

70. Sally Friedman, "Successful, by Design," *Jewish Exponent* (Philadelphia), Dec. 29, 1995, 54.

71. Eleni Sakes Epstein, "Trigère," in *American Fashion*, ed. Sara Tomerlin Lee (New York: Fashion Institute of Technology, 1975), 415, 419.

72. Brady, "Ego, Libido, Genius, Chicanery," 70.

73. Christopher Petkanas, "Fabulous Dead People: Pauline Trigère," *T: The New York Times Style Magazine*, Feb. 28, 2011.

74. Renée Hunter, telephone interview, May 19, 2021, by Kimberly Chrisman-Campbell.

75. *Contemporary Fashion*, ed. Richard Martin and Taryn Benbow-Pfalzgraf, eds., *Contemporary Fashion* (New York: St. James Press, 2002), 651.

76. Zwecker, "Peg Says."

77. Graham, "White House Holds First Fashion Show."

78. Letter, Lynda Johnson Robb to Donald Brooks, Mar. 4, 1968, "Brooks–D," White House Social Files, Alpha File, Box 262, LBJ Library.

79. Strasburg, "Fashion Flies In."

80. Bender, *The Beautiful People*, 132.

81. "Summer Pacesetters Plus and Minus," *Women's Wear Daily*, Feb. 15, 1968.

82. Virginia Pope, "Herbert Kasper, 26, Is Known for Youthful, Sophisticated Styles," *New York Times*, Oct. 5, 1953; Lisa Lockwood, "Herbert Kasper, Fashion Designer, 93," *Women's Wear Daily*, Mar. 4, 2020.

83. "Annual Fashion Critics Award Winners for 1970 Announced," *Baltimore Sun*, June 24, 1970.

84. Memo, Bess Abell to Mildred Stegall, Feb. 26, 1968, "Luncheon (Mrs. Johnson) (Governor's Wives) Thursday, February 29, 1968 at 1:00 pm," White House Social Files, White House Social Entertainment, Box 109, LBJ Library.

85. Lambert, *World of Fashion*, 253.

86. Milbank, *New York Fashion*, 213–14.

87. Barbara Cloud, "Patriotism Style at First White House Fashion Show," *Pittsburgh Press*, Mar. 1, 1968.

88. Lady Bird Johnson's Daily Diary, Feb. 29, 1968, LBJ Library.

89. Cloud, "First and Last White House Fashion Show"; Eleni, *"White House Fashion First*

Waves Flag for U.S. Travel"; Graham, "White House Holds First Fashion Show."

90. Strasburg, "Fashion Flies In."
91. Cable, Luba Marks to Lady Bird Johnson, Feb. 29, 1968, "Luncheon (Mrs. Johnson) (Governor's Wives) Thursday, Feb. 29, 1968 at 1:00 pm," White House Social Files, White House Social Entertainment, Box 109, LBJ Library.
92. Ruth Preston, "Talk about Clothes: Lunch at the White House," *New York Post*, Mar. 1, 1968.
93. *Chicago Daily News*, Mar. 1, 1968.
94. Strasburg, "Fashion Flies In."
95. Lady Bird Johnson's Daily Diary, Feb. 29, 1968, LBJ Library.

6. The Runway

1. Marie Smith, "LBJ's Party Planner: She's Cruise Director for the Ship of State," *Washington Post*, May 7, 1967.
2. Rubye Graham, "White House Holds First Fashion Show," *Philadelphia Inquirer*, Mar. 1, 1968.
3. Eugenia Sheppard, "Fashion Has Its First Big Fling at the White House," *Los Angeles Times*, Mar. 4, 1968.
4. Mary Strasburg, "VIP Wives 'Discover America' . . . The White House Way," *Washington Post*, Mar. 1, 1968; "Happening," *Washington Post*, Mar. 2, 1968.
5. Sherry Thomas, telephone interview, May 14, 2015, by Kimberly Chrisman-Campbell.
6. Peggy Parke Mathieu, telephone interview, July 6, 2017, by Kimberly Chrisman-Campbell.
7. Lynda Hatch, telephone interview, April 19, 2021, by Kimberly Chrisman-Campbell.
8. China Machado, telephone interview, Nov. 12, 2014, by Kimberly Chrisman-Campbell.
9. Renée Hunter, telephone interview, May 19, 2021, by Kimberly Chrisman-Campbell.
10. Myra MacPherson, "Governors' Wives 'Discover America in Style' at White House," *New York Times*, Mar. 1, 1968; Michael L. Gillette, *Lady Bird Johnson: An Oral History* (New York: Oxford Univ. Press, 2012), 364.
11. Jennifer Chillcott Garrigues, telephone interview, May 4, 2021, by Kimberly Chrisman-Campbell.
12. Sheppard, "Fashion Has Its First Big Fling at the White House."
13. Joann Harris, "White House Puts On Fashions," *Baltimore Sun*, Mar. 10, 1968.
14. Remarks of Mrs. Lyndon B. Johnson at Governors' Wives Luncheon, Feb. 29, 1968, "Luncheon (Mrs. Johnson) (Governor's Wives) Thursday, February 29, 1968 at 1:00 pm," White House Social Files, White House Social Entertainment, Box 109, LBJ Library.
15. Katherine Harrington, "Historic Event, Washington Style," *Knickerbocker News* (Albany, NY), Mar. 1, 1968; Ruth Preston, "Talk about Clothes: Lunch at the White House," *New York Post*, Mar. 1, 1968.
16. Remarks of Miss Nancy White, Discover America Fashion Show, Governors' Wives Luncheon, Feb. 29, 1968, "White House Fashion Show, 2/29/1968 [2 of 3]," White House Social Files, Bess Abell Files, Box 23, LBJ Library. All of White's comments in this chapter are taken from this source.
17. Sheppard, "Fashion Has Its First Big Fling at the White House."
18. Frances Spatz Leighton, "It Looked Easy—but It Wasn't!," *Chicago Tribune*, May 5, 1968.
19. Harrington, "Historic Event, Washington Style."
20. Sheppard, "Fashion Has Its First Big Fling at the White House.
21. Transcript, Sharon Francis Oral History Interview I, September 5, 1980, by Dorothy Pierce, AC81–68–71, p. 14, LBJ Library.
22. Harris, "White House Puts On Fashions."
23. Leighton, "It Looked Easy."
24. Harrington, "Historic Event, Washington Style."
25. "Happening," *Washington Post*, Mar. 2, 1968.
26. Peg Zwecker, "Peg Says: White House Show a Hit," *Chicago Daily News*, Mar. 1, 1968; Preston, "Talk about Clothes."
27. The *Los Angeles Times* coined the term, on January 20, 1966.
28. Barbara Cloud, "Fashion Focus," *Pittsburgh Press*, March 5, 1968.

29. Milbank, *New York Fashion*, 204.

30. Milbank, *New York Fashion*, 211.

31. "Summer Profiles," *Women's Wear Daily*, Feb. 6, 1968.

32. Marylou Luther, "Is Europe Fashion Domination Ending?," *Los Angeles Times*, May 20, 1973.

33. "Skirt Lengths: A Spring of Choice and Variety," *Vogue*, Mar. 1, 1968, 118–21.

34. Marian Christy, "Hemlines Are on a Yo-Yo," *Boston Globe*, May 12, 1968.

35. MacPherson, "Governors' Wives 'Discover America in Style.'"

36. *Washington, DC, Star*, Mar. 1, 1968.

37. Eugenia Sheppard, "Somebody Who's Young and Fresh," *Philadelphia Inquirer*, Sept. 3, 1963.

38. Bernadine Morris, "A Young Woman Finds Success by Designing Clothes She Likes," *New York Times*, November 25, 1963.

39. Garrigues interview.

40. "American Spring Collections Report," *Vogue*, Feb. 1, 1968, 132.

41. "Summer Pacesetters Plus and Minus," *Women's Wear Daily*, Feb. 15, 1968.

42. Advertisement for Neiman-Marcus, *Vogue*, Mar. 1, 1968, 15.

43. "Summer Pacesetters Plus and Minus."

44. Eugenia Sheppard, "George Halley Wins First Coty Award," *Austin American*, July 17, 1968.

45. MacPherson, "Governors' Wives 'Discover America in Style.'"

46. Eleni, "White House Fashion First Waves Flag for U.S. Travel," *Evening Star*, Mar. 1, 1968.

47. Harris, "White House Puts On Fashions."

48. Dorothy LeSueur, "Presenting: Fashion's Greatest Show on Earth," *Washington Post*, Jan. 10, 1968.

49. Harris, "White House Puts On Fashions."

50. British Pathé, "Thailand Gay for LBJ," June 1966, ID: 2011.23.

51. "Summer Pacesetters Plus and Minus."

52. Marylin Bender, "Galanos Gives 175 Reasons for Buying Spring Clothes," *New York Times*, Feb. 8, 1968.

53. "Spring Will Be a Little Great This Year," *Vogue*, Feb. 15, 1968, 114; Leila E. B. Hadley, "I'll Take Romance," *Saturday Evening Post*, Apr. 6, 1968, 26.

54. Harris, "White House Puts On Fashions."

55. Lady Bird Audio Diary Transcripts, Feb. 13, 1968, p. 1, LBJ Library, Austin, TX.

56. Bernadine Morris, "No False Eyelashes for Scarlett O'Hara," *New York Times*, Nov. 29, 1967.

57. MacPherson, "Governors' Wives 'Discover America in Style.'"

58. Harris, "White House Puts On Fashions."

59. "Fashion: Up, Up & Away," *Time*, Dec. 1, 1967.

60. MacPherson, "Governors' Wives 'Discover America in Style.'"

61. Bernadine Morris, *The Fashion Makers* (New York: Random House, 1978), 18.

62. "Italian Boutiques: Where the Wild Pyjamas Are," *Vogue*, Mar. 15, 1965, 136–41; "Evening Pyjamas: The New Transparency for Legs," *Vogue*, Apr. 15, 1969, 91.

63. Bill Cunningham, "'Fabulous' Is the Word," *Chicago Tribune*, Apr. 8, 1968.

64. A similar model survives in the Metropolitan Museum of Art, acc. no. 1977.412.61.

65. Harris, "White House Puts On Fashions."

66. As a result, the museum has one of the finest collections of American fashion design in the United States. In addition to Rodgers and Silverman's archive, it holds the archives of Pauline Trigère and George Stavropoulos.

67. Preston, "Talk about Clothes."

68. Strasburg, "VIP Wives 'Discover America.'"

69. "Summer Pacesetters Plus and Minus."

70. Cunningham, "'Fabulous' Is the Word."

71. Enid Nemy, "Gingham Turns Sophisticated," *New York Times*, May 18, 1968.

72. Similar examples in different colorways survive in the Metropolitan Museum of Art (acc. no. 1976.164.4) and the Museum of the City of New York (acc. nos. 72.141.1, 76.106.3).

73. "Elegant Clients Drop Paris and Buy in America," *Philadelphia Inquirer*, March 13, 1968.

74. "Halley Now," *Women's Wear Daily*, June 11, 1970.

75. Jackie White, "George's Girls Look Like Real, Live Girls," *Tennessean* (Nashville), Jan. 11, 1968.

76. Eugenia Sheppard, "Inside Fashion," *Women's Wear Daily*, Mar. 1, 1968; MacPher-

son, "Governors' Wives 'Discover America in Style.'"

77. "Elegant Clients Drop Paris and Buy in America," *Philadelphia Enquirer*, Mar. 13, 1968.

78. See, for example, *Lincoln (NE) Journal Star*, Sept. 12, 1967.

79. Bender, "Galanos Gives 175 Reasons for Buying Spring Clothes."

80. "Summer Pacesetters Plus and Minus."

81. Vintage fashion dealer Vintageous purchased the piece along with several other never-worn Sarmi gowns and samples as part of the estate of Leonard Gold, president of Sarmi's parent company, Nando Couture Ltd.; it was resold and its current whereabouts are unknown.

82. Leighton, "It Looked Easy"; Strasburg, "VIP Wives 'Discover America.'"

83. Preston, "Talk about Clothes."

84. Harrington, "Historic Event, Washington Style."

85. Wauhillau La Hay, "Governors' Wives Ooh and Ah As White House Scores First," *Memphis Press-Scimitar*, Mar. 2, 1968.

86. MacPherson, "Governors' Wives 'Discover America in Style'"; Frances Lewine, "White House Fashion Show Held for Governor's Wives," *Spokane Daily Chronicle*, Mar. 4, 1968.

87. Harris, "White House Puts On Fashions"; *Women's Wear Daily*, Jan. 22, 1968.

88. Strasburg, "VIP Wives 'Discover America.'"

89. Eleni, "White House Fashion First Waves Flag for U.S. Travel."

90. MacPherson, "Governors' Wives 'Discover America in Style'"; Lewine, "White House Fashion Show Held for Governor's Wives."

91. "Mrs. Johnson Promotes 'Americanism' By Fashion," *Palm Beach Post*, Mar. 2, 1968.

92. Eleni, "White House Fashion First Waves Flag for U.S. Travel."

93. MacPherson, "Governors' Wives 'Discover America in Style.'"

94. Harrington, "Historic Event, Washington Style."

95. "Mrs. Johnson Promotes 'Americanism' by Fashion," *Palm Beach Post*, Mar. 2, 1968.

96. Barbara Cloud, "The first and last White House fashion show," *Pittsburgh-Post Gazette*, Mar. 26, 2006.

97. Shannon Rodgers and Jerry Silverman papers, box 8, sub-series 1D, folder 9, Kent State Library Special Collections and Archives, Kent, OH.

98. MacPherson, "Governors' Wives 'Discover America in Style.'"

99. Barbara Cloud, "Patriotism Style at First White House Fashion Show," *Pittsburgh Press*, Mar. 1, 1968.

100. Mary Strasburg, "Fashion Flies In with USA Labels," *Washington Post*, Feb. 29, 1968.

101. Letter, Chester Weinberg to Lady Bird Johnson, n.d., "Weinberg, A–K," White House Social Files, Alpha File, Box 2087, LBJ Library.

102. Mary Strasburg, "See the USA—The Johnson Way," *Washington Post*, Feb. 24, 1968.

103. *Harper's Bazaar*, May 1968, 188–91; Apr. 1968, 5.

104. *Harper's Bazaar*, June 1968, 118; Mar. 1968, 196–97; Feb. 1968, 130–37.

105. Frances Lewine, "Fashion Is White House Guest," *Alton (IL) Evening Telegraph*, Mar. 1, 1968.

106. Letter, Eleanor Lambert Berkson to Lady Bird Johnson, n.d., "Lambert, Miss Eleanor (Only)," White House Social Files, Alpha File, Box 1333, LBJ Library.

107. Letter, Lady Bird Johnson to Eleni Epstein, Mar. 6, 1968, "White House Fashion Show, 2/29/1968 [2 of 3]," White House Social Files, Bess Abell Files, Box 23, LBJ Library.

7. The Politics of Fashion

1. Barbara Cloud, "Patriotism Style at First White House Fashion Show," *Pittsburgh Press*, Mar. 1, 1968.

2. Letter, Eleanor Lambert to Carol Carlyle, Mar. 5, 1968, "White House Fashion Show, 2/29/1968 [2 of 3]," White House Social Files, Bess Abell Files, Box 23, LBJ Library, Austin, TX.

3. Eugenia Sheppard, "Fashion Has Its First Big Fling at the White House," *Los Angeles Times*, Mar. 4, 1968; Eugenia Sheppard, "White House Sets First Style Show," *Los Angeles Times*, Feb. 21, 1968.

4. Cable, Carol Nashe to Lady Bird Johnson, Feb. 23, 1968, "White House Fashion Show, 2/29/1968 [1 of 3]," White House Social Files, Bess Abell Files, Box 23, LBJ Library.
5. Letter, W. H. J. Robertson to Lady Bird Johnson, Mar. 2, 1968, "Fashion show (only)," White House Social Files, Alpha File, Box 767, LBJ Library.
6. Sharon Francis, telephone interview, Nov. 10, 2014, by Kimberly Chrisman-Campbell.
7. See Mark Kurlanski, *1968: The Year That Rocked the World* (New York: Ballantine, 2004), and Brad Zellar, *The 1968 Project: A Nation Coming of Age* (St. Paul: Minnesota Historical Society Press, 2011).
8. Betty Luther Hillman, *Dressing for the Culture Wars: Style and the Politics of Self-Presentation in the 1960s and 1970s* (Lincoln: Univ. of Nebraska Press, 2015), xvii.
9. "Political, Social Factors Enter Fall Dress Picture," *Women's Wear Daily*, Apr. 15, 1968.
10. Hillman, *Dressing for the Culture Wars*, 19.
11. Marylin Bender, "The Fashion Decade: As Hemlines Rose, Barriers Fell," *New York Times*, Dec. 9, 1969.
12. Eugenia Sheppard, "Ruffles Go Out of Style," *Washington Post*, May 24, 1968.
13. "Man à la Mode," *Saturday Evening Post*, Apr. 6, 1968, 30.
14. "Paris Spring Horoscope," *Women's Wear Daily*, Jan. 4, 1968.
15. Caroline Rennolds Milbank, *New York Fashion: The Evolution of American Style* (New York: Harry N. Abrams, 1989), 210.
16. Martha Weinman, "First Ladies—In Fashion, Too?," *New York Times*, Sept. 11, 1960.
17. Lynda Hatch, telephone interview, Apr. 19, 2021, by Kimberly Chrisman-Campbell.
18. Barbara Cloud, "Fashion Focus," *Pittsburgh Press*, Mar. 5, 1968.
19. Barbara Cloud, "The First and Last White House Fashion Show," *Pittsburgh Post-Gazette*, Mar. 25, 2006.
20. Bonnie Pfeifer Evans interview, Apr. 21, 2021, by Kimberly Chrisman-Campbell.
21. Cloud, "Fashion Focus."
22. Sherry Thomas, telephone interview, May 14, 2015, by Kimberly Chrisman-Campbell.
23. Igor Cassini, "Will Princess Muna See Jordan Again?," *Morning Call* (Allentown, PA), Feb. 4, 1973.
24. Bernadine Morris, "Models Try Business World On for Size," *New York Times*, Oct. 23, 1971.
25. Hatch interview.
26. Bernadine Morris, "Indian Story Told Through Fashion," *New York Times*, Dec. 5, 1972; Renée Hunter, telephone interview, May 19, 2021, by Kimberly Chrisman-Campbell.
27. "Fashion: The Accessory Thing," *Vogue*, Nov. 15, 1970, 97; Kathy Larkin, "Focus on Two Young Girls Who Lead a Model Life," *Daily News* (New York), July 11, 1971; Angela Taylor, "Young Models Who Insist They 'Need Something Else to Do,'" *New York Times*, Aug. 31, 1970.
28. Morris, "Models Try Business World On for Size"; Bonnie Miller Rubin, "Sound Eating Habits Help Ex-Model Fight Creeping Pounds," *Minneapolis Star Tribune*, Aug. 25, 1977.
29. "Bailey Rites Held; Was Model," *Baltimore Sun*, Nov. 2, 1975.
30. Dorothy LeSueur, "The Pleasure of Pretty Patterns," *Washington Post*, Feb. 16, 1969; Shelby Hodge, "DISHES on Ice," *Houston Chronicle*, April 25, 1999.
31. Lady Bird Audio Diary Transcripts, June 4, 1968, p. 69, May 4, 1968, p. 6, LBJ Library, Austin, TX (hereafter cited as Audio Diary).
32. Eleanor Lambert, *World of Fashion,: People, Places, Resources* (New York: R. R. Bowker, 1976), 242.
33. See Deborah Riley Draper, writer and director, *Versailles '73: American Runway Revolution* (2012); Robin Givhan, *The Battle of Versailles* (New York: Flatiron, 2015).
34. Ashley Callahan, "Frankie Welch: Americana Fashion Specialist," *Ornament* 35, no. 1 (2011): 29; see also Ashley Callahan, *Frankie Welch's Americana: Fashion, Scarves, and Politics* (Athens: Univ. of Georgia Press, 2022).
35. Transcript of Frankie Welch interview by Richard Norton Smith for the Gerald R. Ford Oral History Project, Sept. 10, 2010, p.

6, Gerald R. Ford Presidential Foundation, Grand Rapids, MI.

36. Winzola McLendon and Scottie Smith, *Don't Quote Me! Washington Newswomen and the Power Society.* New York: Dutton, 1970), 176.

37. Eugenia Sheppard, "George Halley Wins First Coty Award," *Austin American,* July 17, 1968.

38. Milbank, *New York Fashion,* 230; "Norell Left Estate to Friend and Parsons Design School," *New York Times,* Nov. 10, 1972; see also Jeffrey Banks and Doria De La Chappelle, *Norell: Master of American Fashion* (New York: Rizzoli Electa, 2018), 147.

39. Audio Diary, Dec. 9, 1968, 2; Jan. 17, 1969, 1.

40. Russell Baker, "Gloomy Day Casts a Pall Over Inauguration Mood," *New York Times,* Jan. 21, 1969.

41. Audio Diary, Nov. 21, 1968, 10.

42. "The Metamorphosis of Lady Bird; or, How I Learned to Stop Worrying and Love the White House," *Women's Wear Daily,* Oct. 14, 1968.

43. Joann Harris, "White House Puts On Fashions," *Baltimore Sun,* Mar. 10, 1968.

44. Myra MacPherson, "Governors' Wives 'Discover America in Style' at White House," *New York Times,* Mar. 1, 1968.

45. McLendon and Smith, *Don't Quote Me!,* 175.

46. Martha Weinman, "First Ladies—in Fashion, Too?," *New York Times,* Sept. 11, 1960.

47. Transcript, Elizabeth "Liz" Carpenter Oral History Interview, Feb. 2, 1971, by Joe B. Frantz, p. 28, LBJ Library.

48. Maureen Dowd, "Hillary Rodham Clinton Strikes a New Pose and Multiplies Her Images," *New York Times,* Dec. 12, 1993.

49. Bridget Foley, "Obama's McQueen Dress Continues to Stir Debate," *Women's Wear Daily,* Jan. 26, 2011.

50. Vanessa Friedman, "A de la Renta Dress with Many Layers," *New York Times,* Oct. 12, 2014.

Bibliography

Oral Histories

Bess Abell Oral History Interview I. May 28, 1969, by T. H. Baker. Transcript. Lyndon Baines Johnson Presidential Library, Austin, TX.

Bess Abell Oral History Interview II. June 13, 1969, by T. H. Baker. Transcript. Lyndon Baines Johnson Presidential Library, Austin, TX.

Elizabeth "Liz" Carpenter Oral History Interview V. February 2, 1971, by Joe B. Frantz. Transcript. Lyndon Baines Johnson Presidential Library, Austin, TX.

Nancy Dickerson Oral History Interview. August 11, 1972, by Joe B. Frantz, AC 80-5. Transcript. Lyndon Baines Johnson Presidential Library, Austin, TX.

David Evins, by Mildred Finger. Oral History Project of the Fashion Industries: Fashion Institute of Technology. November 16, 1982, 19. Transcript. Fashion Institute of Technology Special Collections and Library, New York.

Sharon Francis Oral History Interview I. September 5, 1980, by Dorothy Pierce McSweeney, AC81–68–71. Transcript. Lyndon Baines Johnson Presidential Library, Austin, TX.

Eleanor Lambert, by Phyllis Feldcamp. Oral History Project of the Fashion Industries: Fashion Institute of Technology. December 8, 1977, 43. Transcript. Fashion Institute of Technology Special Collections and Library, New York.

Stanley Marcus Oral History Interview. November 3, 1969, by Joe B. Frantz, AC75-1. Transcript. Lyndon Baines Johnson Presidential Library, Austin, TX.

Mollie Parnis Oral History Interview. October 13, 1983, by Michael L. Gillette, AC 84-49. Transcript. Lyndon Baines Johnson Presidential Library, Austin, TX.

Frankie Welch interview by Richard Norton Smith for the Gerald R. Ford Oral History Project. September 10, 2010. Transcript. Gerald R. Ford Presidential Foundation, Grand Rapids, MI.

Archival Sources

Nina Hyde Collection, 1914–96. Fashion Institute of Technology Special Collections. New York, NY.

Marylin Bender Papers. Sophia Smith Collection of Women's History. Smith College Libraries. Northampton, MA.

Eleni Epstein Papers, 1948–1991. Columbia Manuscript Collections. State Historical Society of Missouri, Columbia, MO.

Lady Bird Audio Diary Transcript. Lyndon Baines Johnson Presidential Library. Austin, TX.

Governor John Love Papers. Special Collections, Denver Public Library, Denver, CO.

President's Daily Diary. Lyndon Baines Johnson Presidential Library. Austin, TX.

Shannon Rodgers and Jerry Silverman Papers. Kent State Library Special Collections and Archives. Kent, OH.

George Stavropoulos Papers. Kent State Library Special Collections and Archives. Kent, OH.

Pauline Trigère Papers. Kent State Library Special Collections and Archives. Kent, OH.

Washington Star Collection. The People's Archive. Washington, DC, Public Library.

Chester Weinberg Papers. Kellen Design Archives. The New School Archives and Special Collections. New York, NY.

Frankie Welch Collection Photos. Rome Area History Center, Rome, GA.

White House Social Files. Lyndon Baines Johnson Presidential Library, Austin, TX.

Films

British Pathé. *"Thailand Gay for LBJ."* June 1966. ID: 2011.23.

Draper, Deborah Riley, writer and director. *Versailles '73: American Runway Revolution.* Atlanta, GA: Coffee Bluff Pictures, 2012.

White House Naval Photographic Unit. *President Lyndon B. Johnson's Asian Odyssey*, MP 761.

White House Naval Photographic Unit. Outs Roll 11 of 19 from MP 761.

White House Naval Photographic Unit. *The President, February 1968*, MP 893.

White House Naval Photographic Unit. Outs Roll 15 of 16 from MP 893.

White House Naval Photographic Unit. Outs Roll 16 of 16 from MP 893.

White House Naval Photographic Unit. *Faces of the West.* MP 1039.

White House Naval Photographic Unit. Outs Roll 2 of 2 from MP1039.

Articles, Books, and Theses

Banks, Jeffrey and Doria De La Chapelle. *Norell: Master of American Fashion.* New York: Rizzoli Electa, 2018.

Bland, Kasey. "The Life and Career of Fashion Designer George Stavropoulos." MA thesis, University of Akron, 2008.

Brady, James. "Ego, Libido, Genius, Chicanery: The Inside Story of Fashion," *New York Magazine*, November 25, 1974, 69–77.

Becker, Annette. "Mollie Parnis: Tastemaker." In *The Hidden History of American Fashion: Rediscovering 20th-Century Women Designers*, edited by Nancy Deihl, 149–62. New York: Bloomsbury Academic, 2018.

Bender, Marylin. *The Beautiful People.* New York: Coward-McCann, 1967.

Beyer, Rick, and Elizabeth Sayles. *The Ghost Army of World War II: How One Top-Secret Unit Deceived the Enemy with Inflatable Tanks, Sound Effects, and Other Audacious Fakery.* New York: Princeton Architectural Press, 2015.

Blass, Bill. *Bare Blass.* New York: HarperCollins, 2002.

Bradley, Barry W. *Galanos.* Cleveland: Western Reserve Historical Society, 1996.

Callahan, Ashley. "Frankie Welch: Americana Fashion Specialist," *Ornament* 35, no. 1 (2011): 26–31.

———. *Frankie Welch's Americana: Fashion, Scarves, and Politics.* Athens: Univ. of Georgia Press, 2022.

Collins, Amy Fine. "The Lady, The List, The Legacy," *Vanity Fair*, April 2004, 260–71.

———. *The International Best-Dressed List: The Official Story.* New York: Rizzoli, 2019.

Dickerson, John. *On Her Trail: My Mother, Nancy Dickerson, TV News' First Woman Star.* New York: Simon & Schuster, 2006.

Epstein, Eleni Sakes. "Trigère." In *American Fashion*, edited by Sara Tomerlin Lee, 409–96, New York: Fashion Institute of Technology, 1975.

Gillette, Michael L. *Lady Bird Johnson: An Oral History*. New York: Oxford Univ. Press, 2012.

Givhan, Robin. *The Battle of Versailles*. New York: Flatiron, 2015.

Hamilton, George, and William Stadiem. *Don't Mind If I Do*. New York: Touchstone, 2008.

Hillman, Betty Luther. *Dressing for the Culture Wars: Style and the Politics of Self-Presentation in the 1960s and 1970s*. Lincoln: Univ. of Nebraska Press, 2015.

Kurlanski, Mark. *1968: The Year That Rocked the World*. New York: Ballantine, 2004.

Lambert, Eleanor. *World of Fashion: People, Places, Resources*. New York: R. R. Bowker, 1976.

Lane, Kenneth Jay. *Faking It*. New York: Abrams, 1996.

Magidson, Phyllis, and Donald Albrecht, ed. *Mod New York: Fashion Takes a Trip*. New York: Museum of the City of New York and the Monacelli Press, 2017.

Martin, Richard. *American Ingenuity: Sportswear, 1930s–1970s*. New York: Metropolitan Museum of Art, 1998.

Martin, Richard, and Taryn Benbow-Pfalzgraf, eds. *Contemporary Fashion*. New York: St. James Press, 2002.

McLendon, Winzola, and Scottie Smith. *Don't Quote Me! Washington Newswomen and the Power Society*. New York: Dutton, 1970.

Mears, Patricia. *Impact: 50 Years of The Council of Fashion Designers of America*. New York: Abrams, 2012.

Milbank, Caroline Rennolds. *New York Fashion: The Evolution of American Style*. New York: Harry N. Abrams, 1989.

Moore, Booth. *American Runway: 75 Years of Fashion and the Front Row*. New York: Abrams, 2018.

Morris, Bernadine. *The Fashion Makers*. New York: Random House, 1978.

Mower, Sarah, and Anna Wintour. *Oscar: The Style, Inspiration and Life of Oscar de la Renta*. New York: Assouline, 2002.

O'Hagan, Helen, Kathleen Rowold, and Michael Vollbracht. *Bill Blass: An American Designer*. New York: Abrams, 2002.

Parmal, Pamela A. *Geoffrey Beene*. Providence: Rhode Island School of Design Museum of Art, 1997.

Quant, Mary. *Quant by Quant: The Autobiography of Mary Quant*. London: Victoria & Albert Museum, 2018.

Russell, Jan Jarboe. *Lady Bird: A Biography of Mrs. Johnson*. New York: Scribner, 2016.

Sassoon, Vidal. *Vidal: The Autobiography*. London: Pan Books, 2011.

Steele, Valerie. *Women of Fashion: Twentieth Century Designers*. New York: Rizzoli, 1991.

Sweig, Julia. *Lady Bird Johnson: Hiding in Plain Sight*. New York: Random House, 2020.

Tiffany, John. *Eleanor Lambert: Still Here*. New York: Pointed Leaf Press, 2011.

Voss, Kimberly Wilmot, and Lance Speere, "Fashion as Washington Journalism History: Eleni Epstein and Her Three Decades at the Washington Star," *Media History Monographs* 16, no. 3 (2013–14): 1–22.

Zellar, Brad. *1968 Project: A Nation Coming of Age*. St. Paul: Minnesota Historical Society Press, 2011.

Index